Playing and Learning Outdoors

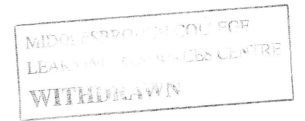

is now a growing appreciation of the importance and value of learning
gh play outdoors.

a world where it is perceived that children can no longer 'play out'
ly and safely, *Playing and Learning Outdoors* shows early years prac-
ners how to pay more attention to making good use of the outdoors for
njoyment, health and education of children from 3 to 5 years.

his book will allow practitioners to develop rich and stimulating outdoor
provision in Early Years settings and enable them to feel confident to
wonderful play experiences outdoors.

laying and Learning Outdoors offers practitioners achievable advice
support, based on approaches which are appropriate and effective for
children's all-round well-being and development. The book includes
cal advice on:

- Movement and physical play
- Playing with sand, natural materials and water
- Plants, living things and growing
- Construction, creative and imaginative play

Filled with advice and support, this lively, inspiring and accessible book
l help practitioners to develop a truly practical and enjoyable approach
o learning through play outdoors.

With over twenty years' experience in education, Jan White is an edu-
ation consultant for Outdoor Provision in the Early Years and is currently
ssociate consultant with Early Excellence and associate lecturer at
heffield Hallam University.

The Nursery World/Routledge Essential Guides for Early Years Practitioners

Books in this series, specially commissioned and written in conjunction with *Nursery World* magazine, address key issues for early years practitioners working in today's nursery and school environments. Each title is packed full of practical activities, support, advice and guidance, all of which is in line with current government early years policy. The authors use their experience and expertise to write accessibly and informatively, emphasising through the use of case studies the practical aspects of the subject, whilst retaining strong theoretical underpinnings throughout.

These titles will encourage the practitioner and student alike to gain greater confidence and authority in their day-to-day work, offering many illustrative examples of good practice, suggestions for further reading and many invaluable resources. For a handy, clear and inspirational guide to understanding the important and practical issues, the early years practitioner or student need look no further than this series.

Titles in the series:

Playing and Learning Outdoors

Making provision for
high-quality experiences in
the outdoor environment

Jan White

Routledge
Taylor & Francis Group

LONDON AND NEW YORK

First published 2008 by Routledge
2 Park Square, Milton Park, Abingdon, Oxon OX14 4RN

Simultaneously published in the USA and Canada
by Routledge
270 Madison Ave, New York, NY 10016

Routledge is an imprint of the Taylor & Francis Group, an informa business

Typeset in Perpetua and Bell Gothic by
Keystroke, 28 High Street, Tettenhall, Wolverhampton
Printed and bound in Great Britain by
TJ International Ltd, Padstow, Cornwall

Disclaimer:
Neither the author nor the publisher can accept any legal responsibility or
liability for any harm arising from the use of the resources and experiences
described in this book.

British Library Cataloguing in Publication Data
A catalogue record for this book is available from the British Library

Library of Congress Cataloging in Publication Data
White, Jan, 1956–
Playing and learning outdoors: making provision for high-quality
experiences in the outdoor environment / Jan White.
p. cm. — (The nursery world/Routledge essential guides for
early years practitioners)
1. Play environments. 2. Outdoor education. 3. Outdoor recreation
for children. 4. Education, Preschool. I. Title.
GV424.5.W45 2007
372.13'84—dc22   2007014023

ISBN 10: 0–415–41210–2 (hbk)
ISBN 10: 0–415–41211–0 (pbk)
ISBN 10: 0–203–93428–8 (ebk)

ISBN 13: 978–0–415–41210–0 (hbk)
ISBN 13: 978–0–415–41211–7 (pbk)
ISBN 13: 978-0–203–93428–9 (ebk)

Contents

Acknowledgements

I would like to acknowledge the most significant of very many experiences over many years that have built the appreciation and understanding represented in this book.

First, thanks to my parents, Jean and John, for giving me access to such excellent childhood play outdoors and to my siblings, Julie and Phil, for being perfect outdoor playmates.

Big thanks to both Jacqui Fynn and Hill End Camp, and to Christine Goldsack and the Sheffield quality development scheme for giving me such inspirational guidance and experiences. Thanks to Learning through Landscapes for a remarkable three and a half years and to the Vision and Values Partnership, especially Marjorie Ouvry who has been a personal inspiration and hero.

Very special thanks go to all the children who have allowed me to watch them at play outside and to the many educators who have shared their practice with me. Particular thanks to the children and parents who have allowed the use of their photographs: Bents Green Preschool; Christchurch CP School; Darnall Community Nursery; Earlham Early Years Centre; Ecclesall Preschool; Jane Wratten; Slinn Street Starters.

And my biggest thanks go to my own children, Laurie and Bryn, for allowing me to have such fun reliving my childhood and to learn so much more in the process.

This book is dedicated to all the children who have shown me how much the outdoors matters to them.

And to all those adults who enjoy sharing children's pleasure with being outside.

Introduction

A child's world is fresh and new and beautiful, full of wonder and excitement. It is our misfortune that for most of us that clear-eyed vision, that true instinct for what is beautiful and awe-inspiring, is dimmed and even lost before we reach adulthood. If I had influence with the good fairy who is supposed to preside over the christening of all children I should ask that her gift to each child in the world be a sense of wonder so indestructible that it would last throughout life, as an unfailing antidote against the boredom and disenchantments of later years, the sterile preoccupation with things that are artificial, the alienation from the sources of our strength.

Rachel Carson (*The Sense of Wonder*, first published in 1956)

The *Shared Vision and Values for Outdoor Provision in the Early Years* (Vision and Values Partnership 2004) states:

- All children have the right to experience and enjoy the essential and special nature of being outdoors.
- Young children thrive and their minds and bodies develop best when they have free access to stimulating outdoor environments for learning through play and real experiences.
- Knowledgeable and enthusiastic adults are crucial to unlocking the potential of outdoors.

Young children need outdoor play. When given the choice, the outdoors is where most children want to be and play outdoors is what they most want. In several surveys carried out over recent years, including those carried out to inform the development of the new Early Years Foundation Stage in England, the outdoors always comes out at the top of children's priorities and favourite things in their nursery. Parents too value it highly and are aware that nursery provision gives their child access to experiences outdoors that they do not otherwise get enough of.

The outdoors offers a perfect companion to provision indoors, working in harmony and providing a complementary environment that enhances and extends what we are able to give children inside. In thinking about outdoor provision, the central idea that we must hold in our minds is that the outdoors is *different* to the indoors; that is why it is necessary in early years provision that successfully meets young children's needs. We need to be very clear about *how* the outdoors differs from the indoors, *why* children benefit from being outside and *why* the outdoors is such a good place for young children's development and learning. Recognising the differences gives us a crystal-clear rationale for putting as much effort into provision and planning for the outdoors as well as the indoors. Just as importantly, this gives us the key for *what* to provide and *how* to plan for the outdoor half of our environment. Knowing what makes the outdoors special and unique provides us with a set of guidelines for making decisions about provision, planning and interacting with children.

Young children have a particular way of interacting with their world and of learning about and from it. They interact and learn through movement and doing, involving their whole body and using it to find out and to express. They take in information through all their senses, with less emphasis on talk than we do as adults. Their brains are like sponges, noticing detail and things that adults miss or filter out. They need real and relevant experiences, with lots of handling, direct contact and playful exploration of materials. They also need lots of opportunities to imitate, repeat and revisit through their own self-directed play. Learning is most successful when children share experiences, with adults and especially with other children. These are all factors we should aim to build into any learning opportunity we provide, whether inside or outside, but the outdoors can be especially effective at offering children experiences in the ways best suited to them.

Play outdoors offers children:

- ▶ Access to space with opportunities to be their natural, exuberant physical and noisy selves;
- ▶ Fresh air and direct experience of how the elements of the weather feel;
- ▶ Contact with natural and living things, to maintain their inborn affinity, curiosity and fascination with all things belonging to the natural world;

- Freedom to be inquisitive, exploratory, adventurous, innovative and messy;
- A vast range of real experiences that are relevant and meaningful and that make sense;
- Endless opportunities for discovery, play and talk so that new experiences can be processed, understood and used;
- An environment that feeds information into all the senses at the same time;
- Involvement with the whole body giving deeply felt meanings and all-round physical health;
- Movement experiences that develop essential structures within the brain and nervous system;
- Emotional and mental well-being, where self-image and esteem grow;
- Social interactions that build relationships, social skills and enjoyment of being with others;
- Lots of opportunities to set themselves challenges and to learn how to keep themselves safe;
- A place that meets the way they learn best and allows them to express feelings, thoughts and ideas in ways more suited to them.

Successful outdoor provision needs as much thought, preparation and planning as provision receives indoors, and there is a great deal to it. Developing effective provision is a slow process that must be done with care and reflection, in manageable bite-sized chunks. It is not at all possible to cover everything about outdoor provision in one small volume, and I have listed several other useful books at the end of this chapter.

Any good recipe consists of wholesome ingredients that blend well together to make a tasty and healthy meal, with expectations about the quality of these ingredients and clear instructions for preparation that draw from tested and trusted techniques. Having spent many years concentrating on provision and practice for outdoor play, I believe there are six major ingredients that make up a full menu of rich and satisfying outdoor provision for young children. I have therefore given a chapter to exploring how each ingredient can best be provided: natural materials, growing and the living world, water, physical play and movement, imagination and creativity, and construction. Each of these ingredients offers highly holistic learning experiences that contribute to all areas of development and learning. Whatever way your curriculum categorises areas of learning, you will see how each ingredient covers them all in the holistic way young children need their learning diet.

In order to offer a complete environment for well-being and learning, we need to offer all six ingredients to some degree, but it is possible to start small with something manageable in each aspect and to gradually develop as confidence and understanding grow. Although the chapters are organised under these main aspects of provision, it is difficult to put provision neatly into boxes and you will find that each interacts and overlaps with most of the others. So, although each chapter stands alone to some extent, you will find more by cross-referencing between them. As an example, dance is an activity that is both physical and creative and there is complementary discussion in both chapters.

For each ingredient of outdoor provision, chapters are organised broadly into:

- ▶ Why this is a main ingredient and what it offers children;
- ▶ How to make provision for this ingredient, with suggestions for good resources;
- ▶ Making the most of this element of provision;
- ▶ Lists of children's books and rhymes that support the theme;
- ▶ Sources of further information and resources.

Just as all good ingredients in a really good recipe have been carefully selected, grown in the best conditions and prepared with reference to the best techniques, another set of themes concerning effective early years practice and how this applies to children's play outdoors weaves throughout the book. Since it would be repetitive to explore each of these for each ingredient, where appropriate I have selected one chapter to go into a particular theme in greater depth, but each issue applies just as much to every ingredient. These themes can be summarised as:

- ▶ Development and learning taking place through a mix of real experience and exploration balanced with lots of play;
- ▶ Working from children's natural interests and motivations as effective provision is child-led;
- ▶ Setting up continuous provision to enable children to self-select and direct their own learning;
- ▶ Storage, containment and organisation as key factors needing careful thought and attention;

▶ Emergent, flexible planning allowing adjustment to make best use of opportunities and spontaneity;

▶ Allowing children plenty of time to explore, play, return and repeat, so that they can get really deeply involved, as essential for effective and satisfying learning;

▶ Engaging parents and carers in what their child is getting from play outdoors and learning from what they know about their child;

▶ Planning based on observation, assessment and evaluation outdoors;

▶ Each element of provision offering holistic experiences with contributions to each area of learning;

▶ Each ingredient of outdoor provision being available in some form in most or all parts of the outdoor space;

▶ The adult role as complex, skilled and sensitively managed;

▶ Challenge as vital for learning and development, and managing risks for both safety and opportunity;

▶ Achieving inclusion by meeting every child's needs as an individual.

I have not had space to deal adequately with such other important issues as the organisation of the transition area between indoors and outside and the role a specific policy for outdoor provision can play in its management. For a closer look at inclusion for children with disability and special needs, I recommend Theresa Casey's book *Inclusive Play* (2005). For more on risk assessment and management read *Too Safe for Their Own Good?* by Jennie Lindon (1999) and refer to the Health and Safety Executive's website www.hse.gov.uk. I also recommend specific risk-assessment training and identification of a staff member with dedicated responsibility for ensuring adequate risk-management procedures are in place and followed at all times. For ongoing inspiration and support for developing outdoor play provision, I strongly recommend that you join Learning through Landscapes' membership support scheme, *Early Years Outdoors*.

Other books deal with design and planning of outdoor spaces. I would advise, however, not to over-plan or designate your outdoor areas and not to split your space into too many subject-specific 'areas'. A basic level of structure in the environment is important for young children and simple zoning can be very useful provided the space remains flexible and dynamic, and elements of provision are not segregated or limited to specific places.

For example, there is no reason why plants, even those for food production, should not be integrated throughout the outdoor space so that children have close, meaningful contact with the natural world as much as possible; and action and movement can and should happen almost everywhere. Your unique arrangement of where and how you offer the ingredients will depend on your own space and priorities.

Because you are using everyday and natural materials, you need to pay close attention to whether they present a hazard in the context they will be used and for the individual children you are working with. As in every aspect of early years provision, children's safety is paramount, and it is the setting's responsibility to ensure that all experiences, whether indoors or outdoors and whether deriving from the contents of this book or from elsewhere, are free from undue or extreme levels of risk of harm. The author and the publishers have made every attempt to draw reader's attention to possibilities of harm and to sensible and effective risk-assessment and management procedures, but this cannot be achieved without active and diligent commitment by practitioners using this book. The author and publishers disclaim any responsibility for how the ideas and suggestions in this book are applied in settings with children.

Everything in this book is underpinned by the thinking and words in the *Shared Vision and Values for Outdoor Provision in the Early Years* (Vision and Values Partnership 2004), which is reproduced in full below. You can add your endorsement to the growing list of supporters for this Vision via Learning though Landscapes' website www.ltl.org.uk

My aim with this book is to help you to create outdoor play provision in which your young children will thrive. With a clear vision of what you want for your children that gives a good sense of direction, a positive attitude to overcome any difficulties and the readiness to make a start, however small, the journey will begin. Once started, it can be a most enjoyable journey, and one that is vitally important for every young child.

I would like to leave you with more wise and highly appropriate words by Rachel Carson, written in 1956 and re-published in the beautiful book *The Sense of Wonder* in 1998:

> *It is not half so important to know as to feel. If facts are the seeds that later produce knowledge and wisdom, then the emotions and impressions of the senses are the fertile soil in which the seeds must grow. The years of early childhood are the time to prepare the soil . . . It is more important to pave the way for the child to want to know than to put him on a diet of facts he is not ready to assimilate.*

CORE VALUES FOR HIGH-QUALITY OUTDOOR EXPERIENCES FOR YOUNG CHILDREN

1. Young children should be outdoors as much as indoors and need a well-designed, well-organised, integrated indoor–outdoor environment, preferably with indoors and outdoors available simultaneously.

Outdoor provision is an essential part of the child's daily environment and life, not an option or an extra. Each half of the indoor–outdoor environment offers significantly different, but complementary, experiences and ways of being to young children. They should be available simultaneously and be experienced in a joined-up way, with each being given equal status and attention for their contribution to young children's well-being, health, stimulation and all areas of development.

Outdoor space must be considered a necessary part of an early years environment, be well thought through and well organised to maximise its value and usability by children and adults, and design and planning must support developmentally appropriate practice, being driven by children's interests and needs.

2. Play is the most important activity for young children outside.

Play is the means through which children find stimulation, well-being and happiness, and is the means through which they grow physically, intellectually and emotionally. Play is the most important thing for children to do outside and the most relevant way of offering learning outdoors. The outdoor environment is very well suited to meeting children's needs for all types of play, building upon first-hand experiences.

3. Outdoor provision can, and must, offer young children experiences which have a lot of meaning to them and are led by the child.

Because of the freedom the outdoors offers to move on a large scale, to be active, noisy and messy and to use all their senses with their whole body, young children engage in the way they most need to explore, make sense of life and express their feeling and ideas. Many young children relate much more strongly to learning offered outdoors rather than indoors.

All areas of learning must be offered through a wide range of holistic experiences, both active and calm, which make the most of what the outdoors has to offer.

Outdoor provision needs to be organised so that children are stimulated, and able, to follow their own interests and needs through play-based activity, giving them independence, self-organisation, participation and empowerment. The adult role is crucial in achieving this effectively.

4. Young children need all the adults around them to understand why outdoor play provision is essential for them, and adults who are committed and able to make its potential available to them.

Young children need practitioners who value and enjoy the outdoors themselves, see the potential and consequences it has for young children's well-being and development, and want to be outside with them. Attitude, understanding, commitment and positive thinking are important, as well as the skills to make the best use of what the outdoors has to offer and to effectively support child-led learning; the adult role outdoors must be as deeply considered as that indoors. Practitioners must be able to recognise, capture and share children's learning outdoors with parents and other people working with the child, so that they too become enthused. Cultural differences in attitude to the outdoors need to be understood and worked with sensitively to reach the best outcomes for children.

5. The outdoor space and curriculum must harness the special nature of the outdoors, to offer children what the indoors cannot. This should be the focus for outdoor provision, complementing and extending provision indoors.

The outdoors offers young children essential experiences vital to their well-being, health and development in all areas. Children who miss these experiences are significantly deprived. Outdoors, children can have the freedom to explore different ways of 'being', feeling, behaving and interacting; they have space – physical (up as well as sideways), mental and emotional; they have room and permission to be active, interactive, messy, noisy and work on a large scale; they may feel less controlled by adults.

The real contact with the elements, seasons and the natural world, the range of perspectives, sensations and environments – multi-dimensional and multi-sensory, and the daily change, uncertainty, surprise and excitement all contribute to the desire young children have to be outside. It cannot be the same indoors; a child cannot be the same indoors – outdoors is a vital, special and deeply engaging place for young children.

6. Outdoors should be a dynamic, flexible and versatile place where children can choose, create, change and be in charge of their play environment.

Outdoor provision can, and should, offer young children an endlessly versatile, changeable and responsive environment for all types of play where they can manipulate, create, control and modify. This offers a huge sense of freedom, which is not readily available indoors. It also underpins the development of creativity and the dispositions for learning. The space itself as well as resources, layout, planning and routines all need to be versatile, open-ended and flexible to maximise their value to the child.

7. Young children must have a rich outdoor environment full of irresistible stimuli, contexts for play, exploration and talk, plenty of real experiences and contact with the natural world and with the community.

Through outdoor play, young children can learn the skills of social interaction and friendship, care for living things and their environment, be curious and fascinated, experience awe, wonder and joy and become 'lost in the experience'. They can satisfy their deep urge to explore, experiment and understand and become aware of their community and locality, thus developing a sense of connection to the physical, natural and human world.

A particular strength of outdoor provision is that it offers children many opportunities to experience the real world, have first-hand experiences, do real tasks and do what adults do, including being involved in the care of the outdoor space. Settings should make the most of this aspect, with connected play opportunities.

An aesthetic awareness of and emotional link to the non-constructed or controlled, multi-sensory and multi-dimensional natural world is a crucial component of human well-being, and increasingly absent in young children's lives. The richness of cultural diversity is an important part of our everyday world; this can and should be explored by children through outdoor experiences. Giving children a sense of belonging to something bigger than the immediate family or setting lays foundations for living as a community.

8. Young children should have long periods of time outside. They need to know that they can be outside every day, when they want to and that they can develop their ideas for play over time.

High-quality play outdoors, where children are deeply involved, only emerges when they know they are not hurried. They need to have time to develop their use of spaces and resources and uninterrupted time to develop their play ideas, or to construct a place and then play in it or to get into problem-solving on a big scale. They need to be able to return to projects again and again until 'finished' with them.

Slow learning is good learning, giving time for assimilation. When children can move between indoors and outside, their play or explorations develop further still. Young children also need time (and places) to day-dream, look on or simply relax outside.

9. Young children need challenge and risk within a framework of security and safety. The outdoor environment lends itself to offering challenge, helping children learn how to be safe and to be aware of others.

Children are seriously disadvantaged if they do not learn how to approach and manage physical and emotional risk. They can become either timid or reckless, or be unable to cope with consequences. Young children need to be able to set and meet their own challenges, become aware of their limits and push their abilities (at their own pace), be prepared to make mistakes, and experience the pleasure of feeling capable and competent. Challenge and its associated risk are vital for this. Young children also need to learn how to recognise and manage risk as life-skills, so as to become able to act safely, for themselves and others.

Safety of young children outdoors is paramount and a culture of 'risk assessment to enable' that permeates every aspect of outdoor provision is vital for all settings. Young children also need to feel secure, nurtured and valued outdoors. This includes clear behavioural boundaries (using rules to enable freedom), nurturing places and times outside and respect for how individual children prefer to play and learn.

10. Outdoor provision must support inclusion and meet the needs of individuals, offering a diverse range of play-based experiences. Young children should participate in decisions and actions affecting their outdoor play.

Provision for learning outdoors is responsive to the needs of very active learners, those who need sensory or language stimulation and those who need space away from others – it makes provision more inclusive and is a vital learning environment. When children's learning styles are valued, their self-image benefits. Boys, who tend to use active learning modes more than girls and until they are older, are particularly disadvantaged by limited outdoor play.

All children need full access to provision outdoors and it is important to know and meet the needs and interests of each child as an individual. Young children react differently to the spaces and experiences available or created, so awareness and flexibility are key to the adult role. Observation and assessment (formative and summative), and intervention for particular support, must be carried out outside. While it is important to ensure the safety of all children, it is equally important to ensure all are sufficiently challenged.

Young children should take an active part in decisions and actions for outdoor provision, big and small. Their perspectives and views are critical and must be sought, and they can take an active role in setting up, clearing away and caring for the outdoor space.

FURTHER INFORMATION AND SUPPORT

Creating a Space to Grow: developing your outdoor learning environment Gail Ryder Richardson (David Fulton 2006)

Early Years Outdoors, Learning through Landscape's support service for all settings with children from birth to five years www.ltl.org.uk or tel. 01962 845811

Exercising Muscles and Minds: outdoor play and the early years curriculum Marjorie Ouvry (National Children's Bureau 2003)

Last Child in the Wood: saving our children from nature-deficit disorder Richard Louv (Algonquin Books of Chapel Hill 2005) [North American]

Let's Go Outside: designing the early childhood playground Tracey Theemes (High/ Scope Press 1999) [North American]

Inclusive Play: practical strategies for working with children aged 3 to 8 Theresa Casey (Paul Chapman 2005)

Outdoor Play: interactive programme for the creation, use and management of outdoor play Clare Warden (Mindstretchers Educational Consultancy 1999) www. mindstretchers.co.uk

Outdoor Play: teaching strategies with young children Jane P. Perry (Teachers College Press 2001) [North American]

Outdoor Play in the Early Years: management and innovation Helen Bilton (David Fulton 2002)

Shared Vision and Values for Outdoor Provision in the Early Years Anon. (Vision and Values Partnership 2004) available as a copyright-free download from www.ltl.org.uk

The Sense of Wonder Rachel Carson, photographs by Nick Kelsh (HarperCollins 1998)

Too Safe for Their Own Good? Helping children learn about risks and lifeskills Jennie Lindon (National Early Years Network 1999) available from the National Children's Bureau

Chapter 1

Providing natural materials outdoors

WHAT THIS CHAPTER IS ABOUT

- ▶ Natural materials and young children's play outdoors
- ▶ What do natural materials offer young children?
- ▶ Good natural materials for exploration and play, and where to get them
- ▶ Providing natural materials outdoors

  - ▶ Providing sand
  - ▶ Providing soil
  - ▶ Providing gravel
  - ▶ Providing other natural materials

- ▶ Resources for use with natural materials
- ▶ Getting the most out of natural materials
- ▶ Children's books, rhymes and songs
- ▶ Further information and resources

drink in the beauty, and think and wonder at the meaning of what you see . . .
Those who contemplate the beauty of the earth find reserves of strength that will
endure as long as life lasts . . . The lasting pleasures of contact with the natural
world are not reserved for scientists but are available to anyone who will place
himself under the influence of earth, sea and sky and their amazing life.

Rachel Carson (*The Sense of Wonder*, 1998)

NATURAL MATERIALS AND YOUNG CHILDREN'S PLAY OUTDOORS

As a child, I spent much of my play outdoors interacting with natural materials, especially with my siblings in our sand pit, which was simply a large hole in the ground filled with builder's sand. We had plans to dig to Australia, or at least to our neighbouring friends' garden; and our dog would enthusiastically help us. I used leaves and stones to make endless meals and I painted all available surfaces with a sloppy mud mixture. I produced rose-petal perfume to sell in tiny bottles, I made patterns with shells, gathered on trips to the seaside and I collected stone and pebble treasure that I thought was attractive or precious. I am convinced that this kind of play contributed to a lifelong love of the natural world and a strong interest in finding out everything about it. As a four year old, my daughter's summer was fully occupied with making innumerable 'concoctions' with substances from the kitchen, such as flour and sugar, and anything she could find in the garden: soil, gravel, leaves, berries, water. She spent long periods of time deeply absorbed in grinding, mixing and decanting. I looked on with delight and marvel at this deeply curious and imaginative child; and the scientist in her was clearly evident. Now, as young adult she has a very enquiring, creative and resourceful approach to life. Again, I'm sure that this play was significant in her development.

Natural materials are some of the best resources you can provide for outdoor play across all areas of learning and well-being. They are easily found; collected from the world around us or inexpensive to buy from many accessible sources. They are easy to store and present in appealing ways to children. Most importantly, they have excellent play value, stimulating and supporting a wide range of play and generating learning across the whole curriculum in a motivational and meaningful way. They are suitable for children at all ages and stages, with increasingly refined possibilities for play as children mature, from simple digging and filling to the complicated steps and tasks involved in making perfume.

We traditionally bring sand, water and other natural materials into the classroom because we know how rich they are as learning materials. However, they can only ever be explored and used in limited ways indoors because of the restraints we need to place on how children make use of them: mess and space limitations tend to contain and constrain play. How much better to take advantage of the freedom and stimulation of the outside environment, where children can:

14

- Interact with the materials with their whole body, without the constraints of a tray;
- Use all their senses with lots of movement and action;
- Work on both large and tiny scales;
- Transport materials to other places and use them in new ways;
- Be relaxed about mess and so be more inventive and creative;
- Make sense of the materials in their natural contexts;
- Have more room to play alongside and with others;
- Feel comfortable about the presence of adults beside them as they play;
- Be stimulated by what is happening in the locality of the play area;
- Experience materials differently each day, as the weather and seasons change.

The beach is by far the environment with most play value for children, so no wonder it is a favourite place to visit! Sand itself is a most magical, entrancing and therapeutic substance. The full menu of sand, water, shells, pebbles, plant material, open sky and weather creates endless possibilities for the combination and interaction of materials. Children can explore, discover, modify, experiment, build and imagine. Creating a beach-like sand area in your outdoor space will introduce a great deal of stimulus and support for well-being and learning in all areas, for all children.

Water adds substantially to the enjoyment and investigative levels of natural materials, and the combination of these two elements is unbeatable. Good risk assessment and daily risk management will open up a huge range of meaningful and satisfying experiences for your children outdoors. Establish codes of use with your children that enable all to benefit from these fabulous resources safely and effectively.

WHAT DO NATURAL MATERIALS OFFER YOUNG CHILDREN?

Natural materials have very high play value and contribute to all major areas of development. As resources for play they are entirely open-ended and can be used in a myriad different ways. They allow children to make sense of the world around them – first through direct contact with its elements and then as play materials for following their own interests and creative ideas. What other educational resource does so much, and for so little expense?

Figure 1.1 Exploring the stuff of the world

A good supply of natural materials can:

▶ Respond to the child's insatiable curiosity to explore the stuff of the world around them. As children explore their world by playing with it, they are asking first, 'What is this and what does it do?' Later this develops into, 'What can I do with this and what can I do here?'

▶ Provide therapeutic play that is emotionally satisfying and supports mental health. Children often spend long periods of time lost in their own worlds as they handle, manipulate, explore and imagine. Natural materials can provide both the landscape for play and the resources for playing there.

▶ Promote awareness and emotional connection to the world around: playing with things that belong to the natural world; experiencing seasonal rhythms; enjoying the aesthetic qualities of natural things. This can lead to a desire to care for, and a lifelong interest in, the natural world.

▶ Encourage the development of sensory systems and sensory

integration. Natural materials are multi-sensory, offering visual, textural, temperature, weight, smell and sound stimuli.

- ▶ Develop intellectual skills. Through observing detail, sorting and classifying, the basic skills of recognising similarities and differences develop. Construction and pattern-making support mathematical thinking for number, size, measurement, shape and position. Using one thing to represent another underpins symbolic thinking and leads to being able to use our symbol systems of words, letters, numbers and musical notation.
- ▶ Develop both fine-manipulative and gross-motor physical skills: through, for example, digging or lifting and carrying heavy items such as logs.
- ▶ Develop imagination and creativity: their truly open-ended nature means they are very versatile and can be used and combined in endless ways and they are excellent for both solitary and shared imaginative play.
- ▶ Develop language through playful interaction; for example, using descriptive language for the properties of materials and hearing adults describe what is happening during exploration and play.

Natural materials are particularly effective at supporting children to explore their schematic interests (schemas). A schema is a pattern of related actions that children repeat over and over, and through which they are working out how the world behaves. Individual children often get quite driven to explore a particular theme and they will be drawn to anything that fits into this idea, allowing them to investigate it further. Research and practice have shown that nearly all children become interested in these ideas at some stage; observing children with this knowledge in mind will show which theme they are currently working on. Schemas help us to make sense of the grand structure of the physical world and children work like scientists, building their own theories and understandings; so this work also builds up thinking and learning mechanisms. Therefore, an environment that gives children many opportunities to explore schemas will be rich in thinking and learning. With plenty of natural materials and good supporting resources available, you are likely to see children burying, hiding and finding objects in sand (enclosure); filling buckets and wheelbarrows with gravel in order to move it around (containing and transporting); making lines, grids and patterns with twigs and shells (connecting, trajectories and grids); collecting, sorting and arranging items (placing and sequencing) and

17

sending pebbles along a length of plastic pipe (going through). Schema-watching becomes fascinating as you come to understand how children are thinking, and these wonderfully versatile materials are full of potential for meeting children's needs.

GOOD NATURAL MATERIALS FOR EXPLORATION AND PLAY, AND WHERE TO GET THEM

Sand and soil

Many *playground equipment* suppliers also supply high-quality play sand. *Aggregate companies* can supply large quantities of good-quality sand: make sure that it is a high-quality grade and suitable for young children's play. Sand that is ground from sandstone can have fine particles that should not be inhaled. Triple-washed silver sand is recommended; the expense is worthwhile as the benefits of providing sand are so high.

High-quality loam topsoil can be purchased in bags at any good garden centre and should be clean from animal pathogens. Larger quantities can be bought by the tonne or half tonne from builder's merchants and this is less likely to be contaminated by dog and cat pathogens than soil from a garden. It is environmentally unsound to use peat-based compost as the bog habitats from which they are extracted are becoming seriously endangered.

Wood: logs, tree trunk slices, sections of branches, sticks and twigs

Your *local council* and *wildlife trusts* have to manage trees or have materials that have been cleared from land they care for, such as branches and trunks. They may be happy to deliver wood from trees they are felling or pruning, so do not be afraid to ask! Alternatively, you might have cottage industries locally that make products from wood and who are willing to supply suitable materials, such as trunk slices and short lengths of branch. Check every piece for sharp points and splinters and teach children how to do the same. Cut off and sand down anything with an unacceptable level of risk. Planking and sections sold for decking also make excellent resources for construction play. *Treeblocks* supply several lovely collections of small natural wooden pieces in canvas bags. Visit www.treeblocks.co.uk

Stone: cobbles, pebbles, slate, gravel

Garden centres and *DIY stores* with garden sections have increasing selections of aggregates, pebbles and interesting large stones for landscaping gardens. *Builder's merchants* can supply gravel and other aggregates by the tonne or half tonne. *Home-making stores* often have small bags of polished pebbles and *pet shops* with aquarium sections supply a variety of interesting gravels and stones for aquaria. Young children are very aware of detail and will find much to explore even within a simple bucket of gravel. Play will be extended by offering a range of sizes, textures, shapes and colours. Children can paint a set of large cobbles with poster paint and coat them with yacht varnish to make further resources for play.

Plants: flowers, petals, herbs, leaves, grass

Flowers and petals make some of the most appealing materials for play. Children might use plant materials to make ephemeral patterns, for decorating constructions and as food for play in dens. Make the most of common weeds growing in your outdoor space or nearby: daisies, dandelions, buttercups, rose petals, cherry blossom; whatever is safe and available at the time. Some of the plants you select to grow will provide materials for play: scented leaves from herbs, grass heads from a meadow, twigs from woody shrubs; make sure you grow enough to generate a renewable supply. Mow grass less often to encourage dandelion and daisy growth and when the grass is mowed, leave the cuttings for a day or two for children to play with it. Be alert to children who are sensitive to it however.

Make sure children have plenty of opportunities to play with big piles of leaves. Visit parks for leaf-play sessions and bring back large quantities for further play and investigations (if dog mess is a problem, collect from the gardens of staff and families). Make colour photocopies of beautiful leaves so that the original colours are retained, then laminate some of the leaves so that they stay fresh for a while.

Seeds: conkers, acorns, sycamore seeds

Take children out on collecting walks and encourage them to collect with their families so that you have plenty. A large collection of conkers offers endless investigative play ideas with buckets, guttering and pulleys, for example. If you plant some of the acorns in individual pots after using them

■ **Figure 1.2** A range of fascinating and multi-sensory materials

in play, you will have baby oak saplings in the spring (protect from hungry squirrels though!). *Hobby shops* and *home-making stores* often have small bags of shells, pebbles, glass nuggets and plant materials for flower arranging: check that these are safe for your children.

Shells, feathers, minerals

It is illegal to remove quantities of shells and pebbles from our beaches, but small collections can be built up over time if families help. Collect a range of types, colours and sizes, from huge to tiny. Aim to provide large quantities of small shells and a few large and special ones. Organise shells in the removable trays of a mobile trolley and provide lots of baskets for sorting them into. There are several sources for small quantities of shells: for example *Early Excellence* in Huddersfield supplies a lovely range of 'special' shells www.earlyexcellence.com. *Mindstretchers* can supply some natural materials, including an excellent set of rocks and minerals www.mind stretchers.co.uk. *The Early Steps* catalogue has a good range of interesting fine aggregates and shells www.tts-group.co.uk. Visit *www.seashells.org and www.seashells.com* websites for information about a huge range of shells, help with identification and lots of clear images (unfortunately they do not ship outside mainland USA).

PROVIDING NATURAL MATERIALS OUTDOORS

Providing sand

Sand is a wonderfully versatile material that is very responsive to individual children's interests, making it an especially important element of early years provision outdoors. Sand areas need to be as big as possible: the bigger they are, the more they will offer. Make them as deep as possible too, for real digging with lots of energy expenditure while making big holes and channels. Children can use their back, stomach and limb muscles, experience the sand with their whole bodies, dig deep and work on a big scale, work collaboratively and add liberal quantities of water. Consider having more than one sand area, as sand provides an excellent impact-absorbing surface and also interacts with other aspects of provision, further increasing the potential for play and exploration. As an example, consider how much sand can enhance play on a climbing frame if children are able to fill buckets to raise or lower with ropes in a simple pulley system.

Taking the indoor sand tray outside is a lot of effort for little gain. It is important to make the most of the differences the outdoors offers so that you extend and complement the range of indoor experiences, especially possibilities arising from scale, mess, movement, the opportunity to transport and changes in sand's behaviour caused by daily weather conditions. Try to make your sand provision like a beach, even if it is small. Use discussions with parents to focus on what your children like to *do* with sand in large play areas and on the beach, and build on this to make suitable provision that supports both well-being and development.

The edges of your sand area will affect how it is used. Edges that are flush with ground level will give easy access for children with limited mobility and allow children to fill and transport loaded wheelbarrows. Sand will spill into the surrounding area but children will be very willing to sweep it up. Raised sides give somewhere to sit and are good for encouraging conversations while dangling bare feet in the sand, and provide good jumping-off points into the sand. They also provide adults with seating while observing or interacting with children's play. For this to happen, the tops must be comfortable to sit on for long periods. In a large sand area, seating and clambering can be provided with a tree trunk or large boulders. Sand can also be sited in a grassed area with softer, slightly sloping edges where it will mingle with the grass, providing a new landscape for small-world play.

With a water supply to the sand area, you can open up a whole new range of investigate possibilities and experiences. Very wet, sloppy sand behaves very differently to damp sand; it is fascinating how water first collects and then drains away; trenches in the sand can be filled to make moving water systems. Very runny sand feels amazing and intriguing sculptures can be made by dripping the sand by hand. Use small sparkly items with very wet sand and shallow pans or sieves for children to try panning for gold!

Sand must be maintained in a condition fit for use. Covering large sand areas is not difficult, but the cover needs to be lightweight, so that it is easy to place and remove, and allow rainwater to drain through. Solid covers reduce the air flow to the sand, making it stagnant, mouldy and attractive to unwanted mini-beasts. Garden centres and builders' yards supply a range of suitable plastic meshes and these can be weighted down with the small tyres provided for play: children will be willing helpers. Animal 'chasers' that emit high-pitched ultrasound to deter dogs, cats and foxes from using the sand or soil at night can now be found in garden catalogues and from several specialist suppliers. Some settings with large beach-like sand areas rely on these as an alternative to covering their sand. When creating the sand area, ensure that drainage of rainwater and water used in play will not be hindered: a layer of gravel under the sand should help, with a robust, permeable landscape membrane to reduce mixing (the advice of a landscape designer for your particular outdoor area can be helpful at this stage; see if any of your parents have this expertise). Encourage deep digging in play to aid aeration and give the sand a deep and thorough flush and turn-over at least once a term. Diluted sterilising agents in the flushing water can also help to keep bacteria and algae at bay. Shade needs to accommodate the movement of the sun, which is most harmful from 12 to 2 pm in high summer. If shade-sails are used, make sure that they filter out harmful UV rays. Sand boxes with roofs often do not provide shade where it is needed, so do select carefully. Your risk assessment for this aspect of provision should include knowledge of your own children, especially sensitive skin and hair and the possibility of a child putting sand in their mouth.

Equipment and opportunities for outdoor sand provision need to complement and extend those offered indoors, rather than replicating them. To make this happen plan for sand experiences across both indoors and outdoors at the same time, making the most of the differences in the two environments. Store twigs, shells, pebbles and other natural materials nearby to encourage their interaction with sand and soil.

It is important not to allow the sand or soil area to become cluttered with resources: cluttering hampers play, especially if the area is small. Every now and then try having no resources at all, so that children interact directly and simply with the material. Sand, especially, is a beautiful, therapeutic substance that can be experienced more fully by sitting or lying in it, with hands and bare feet, feeling the cool and delicate sensations on the skin or trickling it through fingers and toes. Moist sand can be moulded into extensive landscapes with tunnels and roadways, with no need for any items additional to the child's imagination.

Providing soil

Earth really is a special substance that holds many fascinations for young investigators. Children can dig in it, turn it over, bury and re-find artefacts, make holes, fill buckets and wheelbarrows and then refill the hole. Although similar to sand, it looks and behaves differently and also holds the special fascination of creepy-crawlies; so it is worth making provision for both soil and sand if possible. When dry it is hard and crumbly, but when moist it can be moulded with the hands; a good earthy loam also smells wonderful. Mixed with water, it is something else again. Mud itself intrigues as you make marks in it or paint with it, and feels amazing as it oozes between fingers or even toes! It makes excellent pies, stews, potions and brews, with the addition of plant material and stones (see *Nature's Playground* by Danks and Schofield, 2006, pages 52–4). Ensure that cuts, especially deep ones, are covered with a plaster or gloves, to reduce any risk of infection. Compost is a poor substitute for texture and behaviour and does not mix well for mud pies, so do try to give children access to good-quality earthy top-soil.

Ideally, children need to be able to stand in the digging area so that they can dig with long-handled tools and use all their muscles: teach them how to use their feet on a spade for effective digging and an excellent physical workout. If you do not have enough ground available, try using a planter or large tyre (lined with landscape fabric to contain the earth) or make raised beds. Hygiene will be important: keep cats and other animals off with a weighted net, tarpaulin or vented plywood cover (and perhaps an ultrasonic repellent) and ensure children get into the habit of washing hands carefully after play, especially before eating.

Providing gravel

A large quantity of gravel has several play possibilities: as a loose material for filling, pouring and moving, as a landscape for small-world play and as a large number of small items for placing and arranging. Each piece of stone has unique details, which young children are observant enough to distinguish. Close up, the colours are very variable, as are shape and size, allowing for a great deal of sorting and pattern-making. Large play landscapes can be made with railway sleepers; if space allows, try having surfaces at different levels to add to the possibilities for use. Tractor tyres also make good containers (lined with landscape fabric or plastic sheeting with drainage holes). An array of different landscapes can be provided by grouping tyres filled with different aggregates, including sand – try also planting grasses or other robust plants and adding logs and large sculptural rocks. Be alert to the possibility of children putting gravel pieces in their mouths, as they may represent a choking hazard, although settings that provide gravel do not find this to be a problem.

■ Figure 1.3 Sharing ideas with pebbles and stones

Providing other natural materials

Large quantities of small items will rapidly become muddled and difficult to use unless attention is paid to keeping them well organised and appealingly presented. They will be used in a wider range of ways if they are stored in containers that can be taken to different parts of the outdoor area. Selection of a suitable container will depend on the size and weight of the resources, but do make sure that some can be moved by the children themselves. Trolleys with deep and shallow removable trays and vegetable racks can be wheeled to sand, grass or paving – wherever they are needed. Plastic laundry baskets and bread crates make good containers for larger items and can be carried by children working together. Some resources can be left outside in piles or in bins (ensure they have drainage) and a tarpaulin will prevent them becoming dirty from rain-splash. Baskets and clear plastic crates for lightweight resources can be stored on shelving in the outdoor shed. Baskets are a particularly appealing way of presenting smaller natural materials for sorting, classifying and pattern-making, perhaps on a picnic blanket; those with a handle are easier for children to use for transporting. Take close-up photographs and use laminated copies to label containers clearly. Images of children at play may also stimulate ideas for the next user. Supplement large collections of readily available materials with some special items, such as bigger shells with mother of pearl covering. Give plenty of time for children to sort resources back into their containers at the end of play. If materials have got muddled, have a big sort-out together involving much mathematical discussion.

RESOURCES FOR USE WITH NATURAL MATERIALS

Equipment for supporting the use of natural materials needs to capitalise on what the outdoors has to offer that the indoors does not (see above). The right clothing makes all the difference, especially when it is cold. Children need to be comfortable, but there is no reason not to use sand and soil all through the year. With suitable clothing we can capitalise fully on the dynamic nature of the outdoors as the behaviour of sand and soil varies greatly across the year, and children can have the long periods they need for complex and satisfying play. The best resources for this area of provision outdoors allow active, exploratory, inventive and large-scale activity.

RESOURCES FOR USE WITH NATURAL MATERIALS

▶ Transporters such as wheelbarrows, carts and baskets on bikes

▶ Buckets with handles for lifting and carrying

▶ Bags, baskets, tool boxes: anything which can be filled and carried

▶ Long-handled spades, forks, rakes (mostly child-sized with one or two adult-sized)

▶ Child-sized trowels and other hand tools (metal ones are usually more effective than plastic)

▶ Long-handled brooms and a dustpan and brush (sweeping is a very physical activity that children love and they can help to tidy up, returning spilled sand to the sand pit)

▶ Old school kitchen equipment (such as big metal pots and ladles)

▶ Milk and bread crates

▶ Plastic guttering and pipes

▶ Garden sieves

▶ A water supply, hoses and watering cans

▶ Protective clothing such as rain-gear (dungarees provide ideal clothing when it is not raining as they cover tummy and legs while leaving arms free for movement)

▶ Child-sized gardening gloves (for those who cannot have or do not like direct contact with sand and soil)

Just as natural materials are good for supporting play in other areas of provision, many other resources go well with natural materials, especially those for imaginative play:

▶ Small-world animals, such as dinosaurs, wild, farm and domestic animals and mini-beasts – have themed sets ready in easy to carry containers or the trays of a trolley;

▶ Small-world vehicles, especially those that make tracks and with containers to fill;

▶ Planks, small bricks and builders' tools for using sloppy sand 'mortar' and brick-laying;

- A large treasure chest or box, maps and artefacts to bury and find as archaeologists or pirates;
- Something in the play house to represent a cooker and resources to create tables and chairs for a café or pretend snack time;
- Resources for role-play themes, such as camping, pirates or an excavation/construction site;
- Hooks in any nearby walls or fences to make pulley systems with buckets and ropes;
- Den-building resources: natural materials strongly support play in the dens and other constructions children have made.

GETTING THE MOST OUT OF NATURAL MATERIALS

- Remember your own childhood play and share memories as a team: mentioning rose petal perfume usually sets off good memories of playing with natural materials! Ensure all staff realise the importance of children's interactions with natural materials and give sufficient time to discuss and agree both your overall approach and the procedures for ensuring children's safety and well-being.
- Help parents and carers remember and show them photographs, so that they too understand just what is going on through their child's creative play, and be clear about your policies regarding children's safe exposure to natural materials.
- Ensure the children stay comfortable and learn to keep their hands out of their mouth: establish the habit of hand-washing after play and, in particular, ensure hands are clean before eating food.
- Encourage children to use all their senses as appropriate. For example, by bringing children's attention to the smell of materials and the feel of flowers on their cheeks. Encourage barefoot experiences: children have very little opportunity to feel with their feet and yet we seek foot-massage therapies. Grass feels wonderful, as does sand and even mud for the adventurous.
- Observe children's use of natural materials and evaluate observations for possible lines of enquiry or development, so that planning builds on what children want to do and find out about. You will be amazed at the range of possibilities such observations

Figure 1.4 Observe what children do with open-ended resources

reveal (see the example given in *Exercising Muscles and Minds* by Marjorie Ouvry, 2003, page 34 on children's uses of grass cuttings where they threw it, gathered it, sensed it, imagined with it and used it to feed their gerbils).

▶ Having close contact with natural materials will promote awareness and interest in caring for the natural world, provided we also use appropriate opportunities to help children to become aware of the damage we can cause to nature and to treat their environment with respect.

▶ Collect high-quality images from the internet, calendars and postcards and laminate them for use outdoors. Take photos of play and help children to photograph structures or patterns they make: use these to review and extend ideas with children, for display and for home-made books.

▶ Look out for instances where children use the open-ended materials to represent other things, as this kind of thinking is important for cognitive development. Use these records to plan with colleagues how to take this further in a way that retains the playfulness of the activity.

▶ Develop language to describe and appreciate the beauty, shape and properties of the materials. Make a book with colour images and the words you have come up with together, leaving space to add new words as they arise. Develop children's vocabulary of 'doing words' as you describe what they are doing: mix, grind, shake, sieve, dig, bury, find, uncover, reveal, sprinkle, pat, mould, squeeze, squash and so on.

▶ Help children retell and invent stories that incorporate their use of natural materials, such as making the Three Bears' 'porridge' or a story involving a spell mixture that gives special powers. Make most of the potential for small-world imaginative play, using natural materials as both landscapes and play resources, such as houses, caves and tunnels.

▶ Encourage creative ideas for mark-making. For example, with a sloppy sand mix and paint brushes or with mud and sticks, make marks on loose surfaces with twigs or a rake; use wellies to make muddy footprints.

▶ Tell children that they are inventors, engineers, scientists, artists, mathematicians and story-tellers as they play, so that they see the high value you place on their own innate urge to make sense of their world.

▶ Emphasise inventiveness, experimentation and discovery and help children become comfortable about mess. Do not worry about mess yourselves: no creative workshop is tidy while it is in use!

CHILDREN'S BOOKS

A Leaf Named Bud Paula and Sara Shwartz (Rizzoli International 1992)

Billy's Bucket Kes Gray and Garry Parsons (Red Fox 2003)

Body Coverings: feathers Cassie Mayer (Heinemann 2006)

Body Coverings: shells Cassie Mayer (Heinemann 2006)

Carrying (Small world series) Gwenyth Swain (Zero to Ten 1999)

George's Store on the Seashore Francine Bassede (Siphano Picture Books 1999)

Goldilocks and the Three Bears Traditional Tale Liz Pichon (Ladybird 1999)

Grandma's Beach Rosalind Beardshaw (Bloomsbury 2002)

I'm Afraid Too Laura Hambleton (Milet 2001)

Joe's Café Rose Impey (Orchard Picturebooks 1993)

Leaf Man Lois Ehlert (Harcourt Books 2005)

Little Kippers: Sandcastle Mick Inkpen (Hodder Children's Books 1998)

Mummy's Magical Handbag Paulette Bogan (Bloomsbury Children's Books 2005)

One Leaf Fell Tony Speed and Minerva McIntyre (Stewart, Tabori and Chang 1993)

Sharing a Shell Julia Donaldson and Lydia Monks (Macmillan Children's Books 2005)

The Giving Tree Shel Silverstein (HarperCollins 1992)

The Sand Horse Ann Turnbull and Michael Foreman (Red Fox 1989)

RHYMES AND SONGS

Five Big Ice Creams

Five Cream Buns in a Baker's Shop

Five Little Leaves so Bright and Gay

Little Miss Muffet

Mud, Mud, Glorious Mud

Pat-a-cake

We're Going on a Bear Hunt

FURTHER INFORMATION AND RESOURCES

Exercising Muscles and Minds: outdoor play and the early years curriculum Marjorie Ouvry (National Children's Bureau 2003)

Following Children's Interests: resourcing and supporting schemas through outdoor provision Jan White, Early Years Outdoors (September 2005) from Learning through Landscapes www.ltl.org.uk

Playing in the Sand – Naturally Ron King www.communityplaythings.com/c/resources/articles/index.htm (under sand and water play)

Play Using Natural Materials Alison Howe (David Fulton 2005)

Nature's Playground Fiona Danks and Jo Schofield (Frances Lincoln 2006)

The Little Book of Sand and Water Sally Featherstone (Featherstone Education 2002)

The Mud Centre: recapturing childhood Becky Jensen and Julie Bullard www.communityplaythings.com/c/resources/articles/index.htm (under dramatic play)

The Sense of Wonder Rachel Carson and Nick Kelsh (HarperCollins 1998)

Books by the artist *Andy Goldsworthy*, who works with natural materials in the landscape, are truly inspirational; try *Wood* (Harry N Abrams 1996) and *Andy Goldsworthy: a collaboration with nature* (Harry N Abrams 1998)

Calendars and postcards: there are many high-quality images available in card and book shops, such as the *Nouvelles Images* and *Editions du Desastre* ranges

The Pest Control Shop has a range of repellents for sand and soil areas www. pestcontrolshop.co.uk

SUMMARY

- ▶ Sand, soil, stone, shells and plant material form some of the most versatile, multi-sensory and effective materials you can provide for young children. Owing to their variety, properties and open-ended nature they offer very high play value.
- ▶ Outdoors, children can explore natural materials in their real-life context, in fuller and more meaningful contact and in more creative ways.
- ▶ Understanding the value of natural materials for young children is vital and needs also to be conveyed to parents through making their child's learning visible.
- ▶ Staff should agree their attitudes, overall approach and specific procedures for safe use. Careful risk management should aim to open up the stunning potential of these materials while keeping children safe.
- ▶ Sourcing and collecting natural materials is not difficult: they are relatively cheap and often free. Many can be stored outside, needing only a tarpaulin to cover and keep them clean for use.
- ▶ Utilise natural materials both as landscapes and as materials for play, exploration and investigation. Provide natural resources in several places so that they interact with other aspects of outdoor provision.
- ▶ Do not worry about mess: it is part of the creative process and should not be a problem outdoors. Children need clothing that keeps them comfortable while liberating them to get messy.
- ▶ Sand is a vital part of early years provision. Sand provision outdoors should extend indoor provision and be as big and deep as possible. Make provision for children to transport sand and to mix it with water and other materials.

▶ Soil is a beautiful and fascinating substance that enriches children's experiences, so try to make digging available along with gardening. When children can mix soil and water to make mud, a whole new range of possibilities opens up.

▶ The resources that are most effective for supporting play with natural materials are household items and those that also support other elements of provision outside.

Chapter 2

Providing experiences of the living world outdoors

WHAT THIS CHAPTER IS ABOUT

- ▶ Why are experiences of the living world so important?
- ▶ What does growing offer young children?
- ▶ Making provision for growing and natural experiences

  - ▶ Choosing containers and where to site them
  - ▶ Choosing what to grow: what do you want your plants to do?

- ▶ Equipment and resources for growing and investigating wildlife
- ▶ Looking after your plants
- ▶ Getting the most out of growing and the living world with young children
- ▶ Children's books, rhymes and songs
- ▶ Further information and resources

If a child is to keep alive his inborn sense of wonder . . . he needs the companionship of at least one adult who can share it, rediscovering with him the joy, excitement and mystery of the world we live in.

Rachel Carson (*The Sense of Wonder*, 1998)

WHY ARE EXPERIENCES OF THE LIVING WORLD SO IMPORTANT?

Something that is very noticeable about young children is their strong affinity with things from the living world – plants as well as animals. Too many children have little contact with nature in their daily lives, especially where families do not have gardens, or the adults around the child do not recognise or value what it can do for him or her. So a key element of the experience we provide for children in early years settings has to be close, personal contact with the natural world; and this is where your outdoor space can really come into its own. What young children need is 'everyday nature'. That is, plenty of time every day having real and direct, small-scale experiences of the living world around them.

Young children need a multi-sensory environment and plants speak to all the senses, so it is not surprising that plants are such an effective way to improve the environment for learning and play. Growing, especially vegetables and fruit, is a remarkably powerful theme for young children, with a strong emotional element, masses of learning in every aspect of the curriculum, lots of moving and doing and the potential of laying down interests and healthy habits for life. Digging, planting, nurturing, enjoying and eating reaches every part of the child's health and well-being. The living world changes from day to day as the year turns, giving endless new experiences within the predictable rhythms of the seasons and the cycles of life.

When you look closely, the everyday living world is intriguing and magical, and full of awe and wonder: think of the excitement when a child

■ Figure 2.1 Children create the extraordinary out of the ordinary

finds their first ladybird. Young children feel this strongly and we will have done our job if we can help them to retain this through their lives. Just as warm human relationships help to build an emotionally strong core, a connection with nature provides a sense of belonging that contributes to this resilience and offers emotional strategies for coping with stressful times. This will be very helpful for the fast-paced, ever-changing and materialistic lives our children are facing.

Children need outdoor spaces to have soft and enclosed elements in them so that they are nurturing, but for very many settings this is not currently the case. Where outdoor areas are open and hard, high-energy, boisterous play is likely to predominate; the needs of many children will not be met and some may not enjoy the outdoor play on offer. It is very important to also provide places for calm, peacefulness, daydreaming and enjoyment of nature, and plants are great for creating such attractive and sheltered quiet places. It is best to have plants growing all around the outdoor area and not confined to one horticultural or wildlife area, as children benefit from having these elements as integral to the whole space. A major benefit of growing plants on any scale is the wildlife, both big and small, that will live in them. Plants and wildlife can stimulate and support play, and the spontaneous events associated with them add a great deal to the learning potential of the outdoor classroom. Use plants wherever you can: for shade, shelter, boundaries, seating places, play places and for look-ing, smelling, touching, moving amongst and eating. And wherever possible, use plants that children themselves are involved in growing.

Growing is a great way to link home and setting. Parents are often keen for their children to have these experiences and find easy ways to become involved in what their child is doing in the setting. Some children may bring a lot of knowledge from time spent with relatives who are keen on gardening: be sure to use their expertise (and that of the relatives). Do not worry about your own lack of knowledge; it is best to start with something small and manageable and to learn alongside the children. As confidence grows from learning and success, so you can make bigger plans. Everything you try out gives the opportunity for discovery and learning: adopt the attitude that the only 'mistake' is one from which you do not learn! This is a healthy way for children to learn, gives adults the role of facilitators and everyone learns more by finding out together.

Much of the 'added value' of bringing nature into your outdoor area will be highly spontaneous, so it is important to have an approach that can take advantage of these events as they arise. Adults who are observing to capture

35

such opportunities need a planning framework that allows plenty of flexibility, with room for lines of development to emerge. Resources that will support children's predictable interests need to be collected and added to the continuous provision. Above all, children need lots and lots of time outside to have hands-on experiences, to discover and to play.

WHAT DOES GROWING OFFER YOUNG CHILDREN?

- Learning through doing and a wide range of real experiences
- Strong emotional contexts
- Intimate contact with the natural world, giving a deep sense of belonging
- Opportunities for lots of physical activity
- Opportunities for lots of sensory development
- Ways of working in tune with schematic interests (schemas)
- Stimuli for working together, talking and sharing discoveries
- Opportunities to be responsible for the well-being of living things
- Interest in tasting and eating healthy food
- A softer, attractive and pleasant outdoor environment for play
- Foundations for attitudes and interests that can last through life

MAKING PROVISION FOR GROWING AND NATURAL EXPERIENCES

Choosing containers and where to site them

Plants can be grown in even the smallest and most limited outdoor space, and are particularly important if your outdoor space is uninspiring or full of tarmac! Small containers can range from hanging baskets, tractor and car tyres, grow-bags, wooden barrels and old ceramic sinks to dustbins, all manner of recycled containers, such as kitchen pots and metal kettles, wellington boots and ceramic or plastic piping (try asking at your local builders' yard for unwanted ends). Larger beds can be provided with child-height raised beds, small plastic greenhouses (from suppliers or build your own) and borders and patches all the way up to an allotment, on-site or rented from the council. A useful arrangement for young children is to make a patchwork garden by laying eight paving stones in a chessboard arrangement, so that different plants can be grown in each space or individuals can tend a personal spot.

In choosing what container or bed to use and how to set it out for use, there are some important things to consider:

- ▶ Does the container hold enough soil for the size the plant will grow to?
- ▶ Is it deep enough to give the roots room to grow well?
- ▶ Is there enough drainage so that the soil will not be waterlogged?
- ▶ Are all parts of the plant safe for children? (Note that children will quickly learn about thorns and stings; we are concerned about serious harm.)

Figure 2.2 Planting can be deeply absorbing

▶ Can children reach over the whole surface without squashing plants at the front?

▶ Can children with limited mobility reach all the plants to touch and tend?

▶ Can children walk through the bed without treading on plants or compacting the soil (provide stepping stones)?

▶ Is the container/bed in a good place for the plants (amounts of sun, shade and wind exposure)?

▶ Can the container be easily reached by children for watering and tending?

▶ Is the container/bed in a good place for play (will it complement play or will it get in the way of/suffer from other activities such as bikes and balls)?

Choosing what to grow: what do you want your plants to do?

There is huge potential for play and learning from having plants growing in your outdoor space, and so many reasons to grow them. As a whole team, with children and parents too, first have a good think about which aspects of provision you would like to enhance with planting. Then decide which kinds of plants will help with this and where they would best be growing in order to achieve your aspirations. You may have lots of ideas but it is wise to start with something you feel able to manage and to gradually add more planting over time, as confidence and horticultural skills develop. Having made some overall decisions, you can then research and agree on particular plants and placements. Here are some ideas and thoughts to help:

▶ Planting, growing and eating fruit and vegetables offers abundant learning and pleasure. Consult the children so that what you grow is of interest to them and what they will want to eat. For example, peas are tastier than runner beans, although beans are fascinating to grow. Select those that will be ready for harvesting during term time if you close for summer (such as strawberries for June and beans for September). Eating the crop (and finding the seeds) is a good way to set new children's interest off!

▶ Herbs in a kitchen garden have many functions, including being great for children's play stews and potions.

- Flowering plants offer visual enjoyment, smell, shape and texture and will generally enhance the look and atmosphere of your outdoor space. Parents waiting to collect children will enjoy seats placed amongst a flower garden.
- Plants are fantastic for attracting wildlife, from butterflies, insects and spiders to birds and small mammals. Some shrubs and small trees can provide birds with food through autumn and winter, roosting spots in winter and places for nesting in spring.
- A quick-growing special wildflower seed-mix will burst into a stunning summer display that also is a haven for mini-beasts. Choose an early flowering mix if children are not present in August.
- Dandelions, daisies, roses and other flowers that children can pick will be very popular and effective for all sorts of play, such as pattern-making and mixing into 'perfumes'.
- Many plants can be grown for children to play amongst so as to enhance their play. Bamboo and tall grasses, small conifers and shrubs, willow domes and tunnels all provide spaces that feel different and which are excellent stimuli for the imagination; runner beans climbing the shed walls might evoke play about Jack and the Beanstalk.
- Climbers provide attractive cover for shade and shelter; a pergola with climbing plants makes a lovely nurturing and private spot for sharing books or simply chatting. Russian Vine (Mile-a-minute) will provide good coverage very quickly.
- Grouping car tyres piled two and three high, amongst which children can move, is very effective at creating a small planted area, with its own seating provided by the tyres themselves.
- Really effective small-world landscapes are easy to create by growing grass or other small and robust plants in a tyre or even a builder's tray. Tyres have the advantage of providing a warm surface for sitting or leaning on during play.
- Plants can be used to make enclosed spaces or to delineate areas, so breaking up an exposed outdoor space.
- Shrubs provide all-year-round softness and cover for wildlife; perennials offer the interest of returning every year while annuals allow new children to make their own planting and feel a sense of it being their own space.

39

➤ Plant some very tall and fast growing plants, such as maize and sunflowers, so that children can experience their amazing growth from tiny seed to a plant taller than the tallest adult. Lettuce grows so quickly that the whole growing cycle can be witnessed in just a few weeks.

➤ Make a mathematical landscape by planting bulbs in groups and for different heights: growing provides a huge number of other possibilities for building mathematical concepts and language.

➤ Stepping stone pathways through the plants will draw children in, allowing them to have closer contact.

EQUIPMENT AND RESOURCES FOR GROWING AND INVESTIGATING WILDLIFE

Although plants and wildlife will be in many parts of your outdoor space, equipment for gardening and wildlife-watching activities is best located in one well-organised and accessible place, perhaps near to any main growing area. A potting shed will have great appeal, will support gardening work in

Figure 2.3 Intimate contact with the natural world

all weather conditions and may spark off associated imaginative play. Remember that if children can play in it, this will affect what you can store in it. Equipment needs to have designated places so that everyone knows where to find things as they need them. A wooden baton screwed to a nearby wall could provide a place to hook wheelbarrows and other tools. Silhouettes painted onto a wall behind hooks will indicate to children where they should return tools to. Teach children to clean tools before returning them to storage as they will keep longer and are much nicer for the next person to use: children will enjoy washing them too.

Pesticides and herbicides are dangerous in an early years setting and are neither appropriate nor necessary. There is so much more to be learned from the incidence of pests: imagine the drama of a ladybird eating blackfly on the runner beans, and slugs are the most fascinating of creatures! There are many manual and organic methods that will limit pests enough for a suitable crop, and the effects 'pests' have are all part of discovering the living world. Try to make your gardening as wildlife-friendly as possible and use every chance to help children learn how they can take care of their planet.

RESOURCES FOR GROWING AND INVESTIGATING

- ▶ Protective clothing including child-sized gloves for those who cannot or do not want to have direct contact with soil
- ▶ Water supply (make the most of collected rain water and previously used 'grey' water)
- ▶ Long-handled spade, fork, rake, broom (most child-sized with one or two adult-sized)
- ▶ Child- and adult-sized hand tools (metal are more effective than plastic, but they do rust if not kept clean)
- ▶ Wheelbarrows (have several as these will be very popular)
- ▶ Biodegradable pots and seed trays (or use recycled margarine pots etc.) – a variety of sizes increases mathematical potential
- ▶ Peat-free compost and loam top soil
- ▶ Landscape fabric and mulches (bark, pebbles, slate etc.)
- ▶ Canes (tape the ends to protect eyes), twine, plant markers, waterproof pens

▶ Wood for making home-made plant markers at the woodwork bench

▶ Plant feed (buy containers with childproof lids and store out of reach)

▶ A selection of baskets for carrying and transporting seeds, cut flowers, crops etc.

▶ Mat and broom to limit mud taken indoors

▶ Sink or washing up bowl with warm soapy water for hand-washing

▶ Soapy water for cleaning tools before storing

▶ Collecting pots and good-quality magnifiers to look closely at mini-beasts

▶ Telescope and binoculars for watching birds

▶ Cameras and mobile tape recorder

LOOKING AFTER YOUR PLANTS

When considering what and where to grow in your outdoor space, it is important to factor in how the plants will be looked after. The main work-force for this must be the children, and they will quickly and willingly take on this responsibility, making decisions and leading the way: watering, weeding, keeping an eye out for insects, harvesting, sweeping. As adults, our role is to gently hand over these decisions and tasks while supporting children to be successful, to get the most from experiences and to develop a sense of ownership. Think ahead to consider what maintenance will be involved in a project and when things should happen. How about making a calendar of events with the children so they can take charge or let you know when things need doing?

Regular watering is especially important when establishing new plants, through flowering and when fruit is swelling. Plants will weaken if they dry out often or for long, making them susceptible to disease. Conversely, if roots sit for long in waterlogged soil, caused by insufficient drainage and a rainy climate or enthusiastic watering (very likely with young children), your plants will also suffer. To help the situation during summer holidays, water-holding capacity in containers can be much improved by mixing com-post into soil and adding water-holding granules. Water loss by evaporation (and weed growth) can be substantially reduced by laying landscape fabric over the surface and covering this with a mulch. Garden centres now supply many attractive mulching materials that also make good resources for play: take children to help choose those that will be best in your setting.

Clearly, a good water supply from an outdoor tap or water butt will make growing much more manageable, and wherever possible collect rainwater and use waste water from play. It is important to help children understand what a vital, precious and limited resource the world's water is so that they develop habits for its conservation. Let children make decisions about when to water, based on recent weather conditions and provide a really good supply of watering equipment. As well as watering cans, buckets and a hose, try challenging older children to come up with an irrigation system using guttering and pipes.

Small containers soon run out of the minerals and nutrients plants need for healthy growth: enhance levels in the soil when planting and top up with liquid feeds specific to the kind of plant, especially during fruit production (tomatoes especially need this care).

GETTING THE MOST OUT OF GROWING AND THE LIVING WORLD WITH YOUNG CHILDREN

Young children use play to process, practise and experiment with their feelings and understandings of new experiences. It is very important that we plan for plenty of time and opportunities for them to work through all the concrete experiences they are having with plants and living creatures. Although there are many possible follow-up activities, much of this should be through child-directed play. Our role is to find out what has captured interest and to provide a responsive range of play contexts: in addition, much is to be gained by involving the children in setting these up.

Here are some of the ways children might be helped to make deeper sense of all their new experiences:

- ▶ Talk to children as much as possible during and after new experiences, making sure you give time for sharing their fascination and delight: this 'shared thinking' is a very effective way to build understanding.
- ▶ Alongside growing, young children need to simply dig in the earth! Try to provide an area of soil which is big enough for children to stand in to use their whole body with long-handled tools. As well as just digging, they will also find worms,

43

Figure 2.4 Young children need to simply dig the earth

millipedes and woodlice and be able to mix in water to explore mud. Make sure digging areas are clearly marked out so that children can tell where they can dig and where plants are growing, to avoid newly sprouting seeds being dug over!

▶ Take children to visit a garden centre, market, florist or greengrocer as part of the preparations for growing plants, and to give them ideas and roles for pretend play that follows through from planting and harvesting experiences. A simple wooden shed as a basis for such role play will be much more versatile than purpose-made plastic structures.

▶ Offer children opportunities to re-enact an experience repeatedly, such as burying and uncovering plastic vegetables from the digging area.

▶ Bury plastic mini-beasts in the digging area (a large container or builder's tray filled with soil makes a suitable alternative) so that children can search for, collect and return them.

▶ Look for evidence of schema interests amongst your children and make sure they can further investigate them through activities related to your growing projects by having the right kinds of resources available. Examples might be burying and covering seeds and bulbs (envelopment); collecting; filling baskets and buckets with soil or produce (enclosure); transporting these in wheelbarrows and with bikes; weaving in and out between tall plants (going through); watering from a watering can or hose (transporting and trajectories). It is very likely that at any one time, several children will be interested in similar schemas and that they will enjoy playing together because of this.

▶ Many children will become absorbed with gathering flower heads (dandelions and daisies are favourites) and seeds such as acorns and sycamore helicopters. They will then spend long periods using them in pictures and patterns or may use them to represent other things in their imaginative play.

▶ Butterfly and ladybird wings can be made by tying lengths of shiny fabric to a child's wrists (soft ponytail bands are ideal for this) so that children can explore what it is like to be an insect on the wing through running, dancing and swirling: this may also develop into fantasy play.

▶ Natural-world experiences are likely to inspire creative activity with chalk, paint, weaving or sculpture. To avoid breaking the connection with the stimulus, make sure children can access resources and express their ideas outdoors as well as inside.

▶ Help children to become proficient at using a camera so that you can make books to show the sequence of growth of a particular plant, or laminate children's images to make matching and sequencing floor games. Enlarged images could be cut up to make simple puzzles. These can all be very effective ways to allow children to revisit direct experiences in their own time.

▶ Make a collection of fiction and non-fiction books, gardening magazines and catalogues. As evidence of children's abiding interest in the natural world, there are a great many appropriate children's books to share on this theme, so select those that have relevance to the actual experiences your children are having. There are several appropriate themes for home-made story bags with props, such as *Handa's Surprise* (Eileen Brown, 2005) and *Oliver's Vegetables* (Vivan French, 1995), which could be used in a very active way outdoors.

▶ Because of the central importance of growing food in human lives through the ages, many of our traditional songs and rhymes are associated with growing, harvesting, and the creatures with which we share the world. Try asking parents, carers and grandparents to share favourites from their childhood days, so that children can be part of this heritage and learn rhymes from around the world.

▶ Use an area with several containers to create a cosy spot for quiet play: provide blankets, relevant books and selected puppets in baskets to make the perfect outdoor book corner. Snacks will also taste better outdoors amongst the plants that produced them!

▶ Small-world resources are invaluable for providing play opportunities to process prevailing interests from real experiences, which might last for quite a while after the actual event. A wheeled trolley with pull-out trays is just the thing for bringing appropriate sets outside as part of the continuous provision, so that children can play out thoughts and feelings.

▶ Many settings link their indoor and outdoor provision by hatching and keeping caterpillars indoors and then releasing the butterflies into the plants outside. Photographs, information books and the computer all provide a wealth of ways to extend direct experiences and to look for answers to children's endless questions about the living world.

CHILDREN'S BOOKS

After the Storm (and other Percy the Park Keeper Stories) Nick Butterworth (Picture Lions 2003)

A Harvest of Colour Melanie Eclare (Ragged Bears 2005)

Ears and the Secret Song Meryl Doney (Williams B Eerdmans Publishing 1995)

Eddie's Garden and How to Make Things Grow Sarah Garland (Frances Lincoln 2004)

Edward Goes Exploring David Pace (Ladybird Books 1996)

Handa's Surprise Eileen Browne (Walker Books 2005)

Jasper's Beanstalk Nick Butterworth and Mick Inkpen (Hodder Children's Books 1992)

Jody's Beans Malachy Doyle (Walker Books 1999)

Oliver's Vegetables Vivian French (Hodder Children's Books 1995)

One Child One Seed Kathryn Cave in association with Oxfam (Frances Lincoln 2002)

Out and About (Olly and Me) Shirley Hughes (Walker Books 1998)

Seeds Patricia Whitehouse (Raintree 2003)

Snail Trail Ruth Brown (Anderson Press 2000)

Spiders Chris Henwood (Franklin Watts 2003)

Tilda's Seeds Melanie Eclare (Ragged Bears 2006)

The Bad Tempered Ladybird Eric Carle (Puffin Books 2000)

The Gigantic Turnip (book with CD) Aleksei Tolstoy and Niamh Shark (Barefoot Books 1998)

The Tiny Seed Eric Carle (Hamish Hamilton/Puffin 1987)

The Very Busy Spider Eric Carle (Hamish Hamilton 1996)

The Very Hungry Caterpillar Eric Carle (Puffin Books 2002)

Watch it Grow: Pumpkin Barrie Watts (Franklin Watts 2002)

Gardening magazines with lots of full colour images

RHYMES AND SONGS

A useful website for finding the words of traditional songs and rhymes collected especially for the early years is at www.bigeyedowl.co.uk.

An Apple a Day

Autumn Leaves

Cut Thistles in May

Daffy Down Dilly

Dingle Dangle Scarecrow

Falling Leaves

Five Little Peas in a Peapod

Here's the Beehive

Incy Wincy Spider

In Spring I Look Gay

Ladybird, Ladybird

Little Robin Redbreast

Mary, Mary Quite Contrary

Oats and Beans and Barley Grows

One Potato, Two Potato

The Fly Has Married the Bumblebee

The North Wind Doth Blow

FURTHER INFORMATION AND RESOURCES

BBC website www.bbc.co.uk/nature

Ernest Charles suppliers of wildlife-related products www.ernest-charles.com

Gardening tool range for early years from NES Arnold www.nesarnold.co.uk

Garden Organic dedicated schools' website organicgardening.org.uk/schools_organic_network/

Insect Lore suppliers of insects and related educational resources www.insectlore-europe.com

Learning through Landscapes can give a wide range of support through its early years membership scheme www.ltl.org.uk

Mindstretchers for garden and discovery resources www.mindstretchers.co.uk

Naturescape Wildflower Farm catalogue, advice and free visits (Nottinghamshire) www.naturescape.co.uk

Reflections on Learning for enhancing the wildlife value of your outdoor classroom and quick-growing vegetable seed packs www.reflectionsonlearning.co.uk

Royal Society for the Protection of Birds www.rspb.org.uk

Royal Horticultural Society www.rhs.org.uk

Wiggly Wigglers for organic and wildlife gardening products www.wigglywigglers.co.uk

World Wildlife Fund www.wwf.org.uk/shop

Lovely colour photosets of living things from *Phillip Green Educational* are available from NES Arnold www.nesarnold.co.uk

Gardening with Children Beth Richardson (Taunton Press 1998)

Gardening with Children Kim Wilde (Collins 2005)

How to Make a Wildlife Garden Chris Baines (Frances Lincoln 2000)

Minibeasts and More: young children investigating the natural world Roz Garrick (British Association for Early Childhood Education 2006)

The Little Book of Growing Things Sally Featherstone (Featherstone Education 2003)

The Little Book of Living Things Linda Thornton and Pat Brunton (Featherstone Education 2005)

SUMMARY

- Grow plants wherever you can in your outdoor space. Contact with natural world through living things and growing plants is essential for young children's well-being and emotional development; the natural world takes care of children and we must help them take this with them through their lives.
- Growing vegetables and fruit and eating the products contributes to young children's physical health through exercise and diet, and their mental health through building a sense of wonder, belonging and harmony with the natural world. Growing can give children lifelong interests and healthy lifestyle habits.
- Make the most of every opportunity: there is so much potential in every step of the growing process and every interaction with living world.
- The natural world provides a fantastic stimulus for communication as children want to share their discoveries. Learning potential is rich in every aspect of the curriculum.
- Adults do not need to be experts but they do need to be facilitators. It is more fun and learning together is a highly effective teaching strategy.
- There is a huge amount of help available. Take horticultural projects a little step at a time, allowing your confidence to grow.
- Families have a lot to offer settings starting out with growing. This theme is a very effective way for parents/carers to become involved in their children's learning, both in the setting and at home.
- Make the most of your locality to bring children into contact with the natural world all through the year. For example, acorn and conker collecting hold a deep fascination, and playing in huge piles of accumulated leaves in the park may not be easy to provide within the setting.
- Lay the foundations for a caring approach to the planet with an abiding desire to spend time in it and find out more about it.

Chapter 3

Providing for play with water outdoors

WHAT THIS CHAPTER IS ABOUT

▶ Why take water play outdoors?
▶ Providing water outdoors
▶ Clothing for water play
▶ Selecting resources for water play
▶ Storing water play resources
▶ Playing with water in containers
▶ Playing with moving water
▶ Mixing water with other materials
▶ Playing with the rain
▶ Children's books, rhymes and songs
▶ Further information and resources

Through play . . . he adds to his knowledge of the world . . . No experimental scientist has a greater thirst for new facts than an ordinary healthy active child.
Susan Isaacs (*The Nursery Years*, 1929)

WHY TAKE WATER PLAY OUTDOORS?

Water is a magical, intriguing and soothing substance to which young children are strongly drawn and it has always been considered to be an important ingredient of early years provision as a powerful medium for well-being and learning. However, provision indoors usually has to be contained within a water tray and we need to manage activity in order to control splashes and spillage. While there are many good resources for exploring and playing with the water in a tray, children can have contact with it only through their eyes and hands, which limits the sensory information being sent to their developing brain. Practitioners will also have noticed how much children enjoy the feel and look of water coming out of a tap, such as when washing their hands. Running water has even more to offer for play and learning, but this is often quite a challenge to provide for children in an indoor environment.

Offering water outdoors hugely extends the way in which children can interact with and experience it. The greater space offers plenty of freedom for movement and large-scale investigations, and flowing water is easy to provide outdoors. Children can move water from one place to another or see how it can make objects move, and there need be no concern for spills and mess. They can explore how water changes surfaces and substances, being wonderfully inventive and imaginative with their ideas and theories. With suitable clothing, children can play with water throughout the year, interacting with it using their whole body and all their senses. Water is very much part of our everyday lives, and through the weather it affects how each day feels: investigating and exploring water during or after rain is even more multi-sensory and further supports young children in their quest to make sense of the world around them.

PROVIDING WATER OUTDOORS

GENERAL RESOURCES FOR WATER PLAY

- Large closed container for transporting water, perhaps with a wheeled trolley
- Outdoor tap with stop-cock or removable handle
- Hose on reel with connectors for tap and additional hose
- Water butt with secure lid
- Rain clothes and wellington boots for children and adults
- Water trays and large open containers for play

It is important to think about how the water play you offer outdoors builds on and complements the experiences children have indoors in your setting and at home. Sometimes, simply offering similar experiences with a large water container outdoors can be a good starting point, but do encourage the children to make use of this different environment. Children will quickly realise that they can start to fill containers and transport them around the outdoor space because spilling water does not matter in the way it does indoors. They will also realise that they can use the water to cover surfaces or mix with substances such as sand and soil. It is very likely also that they will want to bring things to add them to the water in the tray or to 'wash' them.

In order to provide enough water for these activities, you will need a large closed container to carry the water from indoors – camping suppliers will have a range to choose from. A wheeled porter's trolley for moving crates and boxes helps to make transporting such containers easier and safer.

If children are to make the most of water play outdoors however, settings really need to consider installing an outdoor water tap or running a hose pipe from an indoor tap to the outdoor area, so that plenty of water is easily available everyday, whenever it is wanted. An outdoor water tap is an important fixture to consider when designing new or refurbished provision as it will support several aspects of outdoor provision, especially growing plants. It is useful to include a stop-cock in the indoor piping so that the water supply cannot be turned on from outside out of hours. An alternative is to use a tap that is removable when not in use. Garden centres supply long hoses on reels which can either be fixed to a wall or used on a stand: those with wheels can easily be moved to where they are needed. If necessary, join two long hoses together with a fixing kit, also available at any garden centre, so that your hose can easily reach wherever you need it.

If it is not possible to install a tap or hose, a water butt with a secure lid makes a good alternative. This needs to be raised 30–50cm above the ground so that children can fit containers under the tap to fill them. Because microbes will grow in this water if it is left to stand for more than a couple of days and as children are quite likely to drink it as they play, it is best to fill the butt with fresh tap water for a play session, emptying older water onto your growing plants. Frequent use of the tap by children will build finger strength and dexterity, as well as providing fascination for children interested by rotation and things that turn.

Do not forget the source of water that is often available for fun and finding out, provided by rain! With umbrellas and good rain clothes there are many ways of exploring it directly, or investigating what is left behind after the rain has fallen.

CLOTHING FOR WATER PLAY

In order to keep fully engaged in water play outdoors for any length of time, children need suitable clothing so that they stay comfortable. Since it is children's feet, legs and tummies that get wettest, a combination of wellingtons and dungarees is ideal for most of the year. In hot weather, the best approach is to have some large towels to hand and to ensure children have a change of clothes in the setting. For water play that completely liberates children, try all-in-one rain-suits with hoods. These tend to be lightweight and easy to move in, while allowing children to spray each other or tip water onto their heads. They can also be packed away into a small crate or kit bag for easy storage.

Figure 3.1 Suitable clothing liberates children's play

SELECTING RESOURCES FOR WATER PLAY

There are many resources that can enhance children's explorations of water outdoors. Keep reminding yourself about what is special about the outdoors that is not available or possible indoors (such as space, scale, movement, mess and stimuli from the real world), so that what you offer extends indoor water play provision, rather than duplicating it. As the seasons and the weather change over the year, water will feel different and activities are likely to be influenced, constantly adding new dimensions. Some resources need to be available outdoors all the time, as part of continuous provision, so that children can always have opportunities to :

- ▶ Experience water in containers;
- ▶ Investigate flowing water;
- ▶ Mix water with other things;
- ▶ Respond to the rain.

For each of these, the resources you provide can be gradually developed over time, so that children's explorations, thinking and understanding can grow.

STORING WATER PLAY RESOURCES

Give some thought to the best way to store and present your water play resources so that children have good access to them as the need arises. Lengths of guttering and piping are effectively stored in a plastic dustbin (drainage holes in the base will be needed). A wheeled trolley with deep wire-mesh baskets will make resources visible while allowing them to drain and dry off. If you use plastic crates, drill some holes for drainage and leave lids off until the contents have dried, to avoid the growth of mould. Plastic laundry baskets also make suitable containers, but do not put too much in each one as the contents can easily become jumbled. Laminated photographs can be used to label containers so that resources stay well organised. If possible store these resources close to where water play will usually take place. Frequent washing of water play resources with an appropriate disinfectant solution, such as Milton, is recommended.

PLAYING WITH WATER IN CONTAINERS

RESOURCES FOR WATER PLAY IN CONTAINERS

- ▶ A wide range of brushes, from fine to wallpaper
- ▶ Emulsion paint rollers and tray
- ▶ Sturdy two-step ladder

> Spray bottles, sponges, cloths, drying 'leather'

> Kitchen and/or camping utensils – cups, bowls, pots and pans, colander, ladle etc.

> Buckets and a wide range of other containers, some with handles

> Wheelbarrow

> Washing up bowls, baby bath and laundry baskets

> Dolls, doll or baby clothes, washing line and a variety of pegs

> Builder's tray or grow-bag tray

> Paddling pool

The simplest way to offer water play outdoors is to provide children with brushes and a bucket of water. Despite its simplicity, this interaction with water is deeply absorbing for young children as it gives them opportunities to explore their world in detail and find out how things behave: many adults will remember doing this themselves, suggesting that this activity has significant emotional content for the child. We can give children permission to 'paint' anywhere and everything outdoors and can, over time, provide a wide range of utensils with which to work. Collect brushes of all dimensions, especially decorator's brushes from DIY stores: from very fine to huge wallpaper brushes that need two hands. Offer rollers and emulsion paint trays, sponges and spray bottles (these come with a variety of spray mechanisms to further develop skills and use). This activity is also greatly enhanced, especially for boys, by providing a sturdy, two-step ladder so that children can reach high up. An all-in-one waterproof 'decorator's suit' would add further to the role-play possibilities.

Children will paint all surfaces available, such as bricks and tarmac. Wood, tyres, chalkboard and slate surfaces are particularly fascinating since they change colour and texture as they are made wet and as they dry. If possible, try adding more types of surface to your outdoor space. Observe children closely to find out more about what interests them in this 'painting' activity: some will be applying their current schema or mark-making interests and you will see ways to develop their thinking further.

Provide a large water-filled container outdoors with big kitchen utensils or camping pots (you could try to obtain some old school kitchen utensils such as ladles and colanders) so that children can use all their knowledge from the water tray indoors and apply it in a larger, freer scale. Try having more than one large container or water-tray some distance apart and supply lots of buckets and other containers, so that children can transport water between them: a wheelbarrow will help too. If you have an outdoor water supply then children can be challenged to fill these containers using a variety of methods, such as with jugs, buckets, watering cans, hoses, pipes or gutters: children who love to transport things will find this highly engaging and it will also save you a laborious task.

Washing dolls, baby clothes and bikes or other outdoor equipment are all very popular activities with young children: supply washing up bowls, a baby bath, laundry baskets, suds, sponges and cloths, a washing line and pegs. These explorations are full of opportunities for language development and can develop into role-play themes with embedded literacy activities, such as filling in a booking form and making tickets for a car wash. Boys have been found to be much more likely to engage in mark-making through these motivational contexts. Make a collection of relevant books to share with children and develop the play and learning according to the interests

Figure 3.2 Through interaction with water, young children explore their world in detail

children show (see *Exercising Muscles and Minds* by Marjorie Ouvry, 2003, page 67, for a plan based on *Mrs Mopple's Washing Line* (Hewitt, 1994)).

Children love to put their feet in water, with and without shoes on. Builder's trays make wonderful puddles when rain is not available. Two boys at Darnall Community Nursery were observed by delighted practitioners to perform a spontaneous dance routine by alternately stomping in a water-filled builder's tray, one responding to the other. A paddling pool offers the opportunity to dip bared feet in this lovely, therapeutic substance at any time of the year, as well as making a good rock pool or imaginary ocean.

PLAYING WITH MOVING WATER

RESOURCES FOR MOVING WATER PLAY

▶ Watering cans (variety of sizes and spouts)

▶ 25–30m hose and reel

▶ Hose attachments, shower hose and head

▶ Guttering and down-pipes, pond hose (1in diameter)

▶ Down-pipe hopper, gutter and pipe connectors

▶ Trellis, crates, string

▶ Shower curtain or big plastic sheet, umbrellas

▶ Long-handled brooms (child- and adult-sized)

When water flows it has additional and intriguing properties. It has a very sensory feel, it catches and reflects light, it moves in a variety of ways and it has the amazing ability to make other things move. Running water has a huge potential for investigation, experimentation and problem-solving, especially for young children absorbed by lines (trajectories), movement and enclosure. Exploring moving water in a playful way will help children to get to grips with some of the big questions about how the world works, including how substances behave in a world filled with gravity.

The first area of fascination is with watering cans – provide a range of sizes and spouts, including some with spray ends. Cans with fine open ends (for indoor houseplants) are likely to be used to mark-make on paving and tarmac as children realise they can control the water flow to make trails, patterns and emergent letter shapes. Children will also willingly take responsibility for keeping growing plants watered (make sure plant containers have good drainage!).

Hose pipes come with sets of attachments so that a variety of effects can be produced, from gentle sprinkler and spray to forceful jet; you can also try linking in a shower head. There is nothing quite like hose play on a hot day, but this can take place throughout the year with all-in-one rain-suits. The child handling the hose can gain from the feeling of being in control, which can be especially good for the more withdrawn child, while others can enjoy the sensation of water covering or enclosing their body: clear boundaries need to be in place about who and where gets wet! Try draping a clear shower curtain or large piece of plastic sheeting over your climbing frame so that children can paint or spray on both sides with water or runny paint and watch the coloured drips make their way down the surface. With a hose pipe this can turn into an experience akin to being under a waterfall; try it with big umbrellas too.

Because of the space available, water can be moved on a grand scale outdoors. Cut household guttering and down-pipes (available from DIY centres) into shorter lengths of approximately one metre with a strong hacksaw and smooth the rough ends with coarse sandpaper. These become versatile resources with many uses other than water play and are easily stored outside. Because of their size, children need to collaborate and work together in order to achieve their plans; so these experiences are effective in supporting personal and social development too. Boys are particularly drawn to this kind of play, finding explorations and challenges to maintain interest over considerable periods of time (see *Playing in the Gutters* by Sue Dinwiddie). Provide resources such as milk crates to make ramps for the pipes, garden trellis so that a range of angles can be made and string so that guttering and pipes can be attached to fences. Extend the play over time by introducing additional resources, such as down-pipe hoppers and Y-connections, and new problems to solve, such as moving plastic ducks with the water flow, making dams or getting a water supply from the tap to the growing plants.

Children will also show a fascination for where the water drains to and where it goes from there, so theories can be developed as to why it runs down some slopes but not others, why it collects in some places but not others, and children might enjoy creating a group story about where the water has gone and what it is meeting under the ground. At this age, all ideas and theories are equally valid as we most want children to ask questions and theorise imaginatively; the more creative the better! Provide long-handled brooms as many children will enjoy sweeping collected water and helping it on its way.

There are many commercial water features which can be installed in early years gardens and these work particularly well as part of a quiet area designed for sensory and reflective activities. Remember that young children may drink the water so a mechanism to clean water that is recycled, such as ultra-sound, will need to be considered.

MIXING WATER WITH OTHER MATERIALS

RESOURCES FOR MIXING WATER WITH OTHER MATERIALS

- Sand
- Soil
- Baking and cooking equipment, kitchen utensils
- Small containers and bottles
- Special items such as pestle and mortar, meat baster, ice-cream server
- Plasterer's tools for use with 'mortar'
- Soap flakes, bubble mix, washing up liquid
- Bubble wands, whisks, sieves

Figure 3.3
A scientist at work in a 'mud kitchen'

A SPECIAL BOX OF EQUIPMENT FOR MAKING PIES, STEWS AND PERFUMES

▶ A range of baking trays and tins, small saucepans

▶ Jugs, colander, large and small bowls

▶ Household items: spoons, whisks, masher, ladle, ice-cream server

▶ Turkey baster, pipettes, funnels

▶ Sieves and strainers, measuring sets, pastry cutters

▶ Small paint brush, egg brush, lolly sticks

▶ Egg cups and very small bowls

▶ Small bottles (food colouring bottles are ideal), sauce bottles

▶ Pots of all shapes and sizes

▶ Small and large flower pots

▶ Pestle and mortar

▶ Rolling pin and board

▶ Wire cooling tray

▶ Picnicware, tray

▶ Treasure (for garnishing)

▶ Magnifying glasses

It is important that children have the opportunity to mix water with other substances they find outdoors: both the process and the products of mixing water and sand, soil, flowers or leaves are therapeutic and fascinating, and can support imaginative play in some lovely ways. Many practitioners experience a warm glow when they recall making mud pies, stews, potions and rose-petal perfume and this is clearly beneficial activity for young children. Sand mixed with water makes a 'mortar' which can be used to build with small bricks or to 're-point' the walls. Three year-old children are drawn to the basic activity of mixing such 'concoctions' and this can develop in terms of complexity and the skills involved over the pre-school years, building to grinding, sieving and siphoning. Practitioners need to identify and value the learning involved in such activity, convey this to parents and carers so that they understand the many benefits of this messy activity and organise provision so that it is manageable for all. The best supporting resources can be collected from kitchen equipment such as mixing bowls, baking equipment, a turkey baster, a pestle and mortar, small bottles, spatulas and wooden spoons. Whenever you introduce a new item, observe closely and work with the children to see how they make use of it and to teach them safe use. Keep these resources in a labelled container and ask children to use soil from the digging area rather than from plant beds, and to return mixtures to this area when they have finished.

A whole new area for fascination, investigation and fun is also opened up by adding bubble mix or washing-up liquid to water or using soap flakes (such as Lux) to make 'gloop': provide bubble wands, whisks and sieves.

PLAYING WITH THE RAIN

RESOURCES FOR RAIN PLAY

- Rainwear, wellies
- Large and small umbrellas
- Builder's tray
- Paint, plastic sheets, chalk
- Containers for collecting rainwater
- Brooms, brushes, bikes
- Tarpaulin, tents, gazebo
- Big plastic containers, wooden and metal spoons
- Waterproof camera, dictaphone

With a climate that so often results in rain we need to have a very positive attitude to it! Children love the rain and will delight in any opportunity to play in it or with it. The key that unlocks this wonderful resource is for every child and adult to have suitable clothing, combined with enthusiasm from staff that matches the children's. Water play is a great way to make the most of a rainy day and all the previously mentioned ways to interact with water will be more multi-sensory and have more meaning for young children if they can carry them out while it is raining!

While rain is falling, encourage children to feel the drops on their hands, face and tongue. Given permission, many children will revel in the feeling

Figure 3.4 Young children love the rain!

of gutter overspill on their heads – for those who want to stay dry supply umbrellas. Jumping in and over puddles is exhilarating, as is sweeping puddle water. Try putting poster paint into a puddle so that children can ride bikes through it to make patterns on the tarmac (a squirt of washing up liquid in the paint will help it to disperse afterwards). Painting onto a large sheet of plastic while it is raining is great fun and produces fascinating effects as the rain makes the paint run. Give children chalk too to make marks on wet surfaces and in puddles.

Watch raindrops fall onto different surfaces, both vertical and horizontal, and see how the water runs, disappears or stays: discuss ideas about why this is and where the rain has gone, being as imaginative as possible. Watch the patterns raindrops make when they fall into puddles; this is particularly effective in a builder's tray against the black background. Work out how the rain makes its way from roofs to drain via the guttering and down-pipes; and where it might go from there. Offer children a camera (a waterproof single-use type) to record the images and patterns that interest them – compile a book with the results and add children's comments. Listen to, and perhaps record, the sound the rain makes on windows, roofs, leaves, the climbing frame and umbrellas and to the gurgles in guttering pipes. This can be enhanced by setting up a tarpaulin, tent or gazebo (or simply a parasol umbrella), so that a group can be cosily underneath together – have a snack, tell a story or make a rain dance by patting different parts of the body and stamping. Big plastic containers can become drums with wooden spoons as drumsticks so that children can respond to the sounds and feelings of the rain, either under the tarpaulin or out in the open.

After rainfall, find out where the rain has collected and what it has done to things in the outdoor area. As the ground dries, use this water to make marks and patterns with brushes, brooms, feet and wheels. Children will love to help to wipe wet equipment dry, enjoying the responsibility and learning more about how materials behave in this fascinating world of ours. Some children might want to devise a way of collecting rainwater so that it goes onto the plants they are growing next time it rains. Help children understand that water is a limited and precious resource for the planet. Take every opportunity too to experience and investigate other forms of water that the weather brings us: dew, frost, ice and snow.

CHILDREN'S BOOKS

A Walk by the River Sally Hewitt (Franklin Watts 2005)

Brilliant Boats Tony Mitton and Ant Parker (Kingfisher 2002)

Coral Goes Swimming Simon Puttock and Stephen Lambert (Hodder Children's Books 2000)

Mr Archimedes' Bath Pamela Allen (Puffin 1994)

Mr Grumpy's Outing John Burningham (Puffin 1978)

Mrs Mopple's Washing Line A Hewitt (Red Fox 1994)

Mrs Wishy-Washy and Splishy Sploshy Day Joy Cowley and Elizabeth Fuller (Shortland 2001)

Noah's Ark and Other Stories Selina Hastings (Dorling Kindersley 1996)

One World Michael Foreman (Anderson Press 1990)

Splosh! Mick Inkpen (Hodder Children's Books, Little Kippers 1998)

Squeaky Clean Simon Puttock and Mary Mcquillan (Red Fox 2001)

The Drop Goes Plop: a first look at the water cycle Sam Goodwin (Hodder Wayland 1998)

The Journey Scott Mann and Neil Griffiths (Storysack Ltd 2001)

The World Around Us: what is an ocean? Monica Hughes (Harcourt Education 2005)

Washing! (Small world series) Gwenyth Swain (Zero to Ten 2005)

Washing Line Jez Alborough (Walker books 1993)

Water: exploring the science of everyday materials Nicola Edwards and Jane Harris (A&C Black 1999)

Wet World Norma Simon (Walker Books 1995)

What Is Weather: rain Miranda Ashwell and Andy Owen (Heinmann Library 1999)

Who Sank the Boat? Pamela Allen (Puffin 1988)

RHYMES AND SONGS

Ding Dong Bell, Pussy's in the Well

Dr Foster Went to Gloucester

Five Little Speckled Frogs

I'm a Little Teapot

Incy Wincy Spider

It's Raining, It's Pouring

Jack and Jill Went up the Hill

Rain on the Green Grass

Rain, Rain, Go Away

Row, Row, Row Your Boat

The Day I Went to Sea

The Rain in Spain

FURTHER INFORMATION AND RESOURCES

Exercising Muscles and Minds: outdoor play and the early years curriculum Marjorie Ouvry (National Children's Bureau 2003)

Playing in the Gutters: enhancing children's cognitive and social play Sue Dinwiddie www.communityplaythings.com/c/resources/articles/index.htm (under sand and water play)

Early Excellence has a range of water play resources www.earlyexcellence.com

Learning through Landscapes can supply members with information about rain wear suppliers www.ltl.org.uk

Mindstretchers supplies high-quality rain wear and other resources for 'walking, running and splashing' www.mindstretchers.co.uk

Oxfam teachers' site for information and resources looking at the role of water in people's lives around the world www.oxfam.org.uk/coolplanet

Water Aid website with information and resources about the role of water in the lives of children around the world www.wateraid.org.uk/uk/learn_zone. Water Aid offers *Water Splash*, a teaching pack for the early years with an accompanying set of eight colour posters, both downloadable from the website

SUMMARY

- Water is fascinating, therapeutic and full of potential for young children's learning and is therefore a major ingredient for every setting's continuous provision outdoors.
- Water play can be endlessly and deeply interesting for young children, giving them strong experiences in all areas of learning and development.
- Suitable water-proof clothing and adult enthusiasm are key to successful and effective water play outdoors.
- Outdoor water play needs to make the most of the special nature of the outdoors, complementing and extending experiences children have indoors and at home.
- Water play outdoors can take a wide range of forms and can be offered throughout the year.
- Young children love rain: make the most of the rain itself and enhance water play by making it available on rainy days.
- Continuous provision outdoors is most effective when children can always have opportunities to experience water in containers, investigate flowing water, mix water with other things and respond to the rain.
- It is important to notice, value and share the wide range of learning taking place for individuals while they are engaged in outdoor water play: children will show us a great deal about their competencies, interests and development through this play.

Chapter 4

Providing for physical play and movement outdoors

WHAT THIS CHAPTER IS ABOUT

- ► Why do young children need movement play?
- ► What do movement and physical activity do for young children?
- ► What movement experiences do young children need in their outdoor play?
- ► Providing opportunities for the full range of physical and movement experiences

    - ► Features to encourage movement and physical activity
    - ► Good resources for physical play and what children might do with them

- ► Health and safety considerations: managing risk, providing challenge
- ► Children's books, rhymes and music
- ► Further information and resources

Children want space at all ages. But from the age of one to seven, space, that is ample space, is almost as much wanted as food and air. To move to run, to find things out by new movement, to feel one's life in every limb, that is the life of early childhood.

Margaret McMillan (*The Nursery School*, 1930)

WHY DO YOUNG CHILDREN NEED MOVEMENT PLAY?

Young children absolutely love to move and are driven to develop their physical abilities from birth onwards. They also have great motivation to join in with others, both children and adults, and older children are a great stimulus for younger ones. This drive for movement is perhaps so strong because of its fundamental influence on all other aspects of a child's life, but modern life is not conducive to giving children anywhere near enough of the physical experiences they must have for health and happiness, now and in their futures. Early years settings play an increasingly important role in giving children both the amount of movement and the range of physical experiences they need, and the outdoor space can be a highly effective place to provide this.

For many settings, activities for physical development form the main use of the outdoor space, recognising the greater freedoms this environment offers. But as effective practitioners we must really explore what young children gain from movement and why, so that we can broaden out and deepen provision in this area to fully meet developmental needs across all aspects of physical, emotional and mental health, and recognise the central role of movement in brain-building and learning. It is vital that we offer children lots of time and lots of movement experiences, and it is also important that we work with the child's own drives and interests, that they move forward at their own pace and that all physical experiences are enjoyable and full of play. Young children seem to intuitively know what their body needs, and it is the child's joy and satisfaction in movement that is our purpose and our delight to witness.

Take a little time now to remember what physical experiences you loved and sought out when you were young: getting giddy, walking along walls and jumping off, climbing high so you could see 'forever', swings and see-saws, walking backwards, skipping with friends, rough and tumble play with siblings. All these had significance for the development of your growing brain and sensory systems, which is perhaps why you enjoyed them and wanted to engage in them again and again. Young children are developing a vast array of physical abilities at a pace that is never matched in later life: 50 per cent of a child's learning happens in the first five years. 'Inefficient movement' is harder to rectify later than other kinds of learning delays and movement itself affects so much else about children's development, not least their self-image and feelings of self-worth.

WHAT DO MOVEMENT AND PHYSICAL ACTIVITY DO FOR YOUNG CHILDREN?

Through playful movement and physical activity the child can explore who they are, how the world works and how they fit into it. Through movement the young child can get a real sense of their own body and derive great pleasure in mastering new abilities – and experience considerable frustration and determination in getting there! They can also work out how to operate in a world full of gravity and objects. Movement seems to play a big role in building relationships, starting with being rocked by a parent or carer and developing into active play with other children who become friends. A close look at the roles movement and action play shows just how important this aspect of provision is.

Mental health through the joy of movement:

- ▶ Movement actually makes the brain feel alert and energised: feeling 'life in every limb'.
- ▶ Children enjoy the feeling of their body and what it can do gives feelings of pleasure.
- ▶ Mental well-being develops through experiencing the joy of moving and from satisfying the strong urge to explore movement.

Figure 4.1 Young children absolutely love to move

- Self-image and self-confidence grow through mastering new abilities, especially when others show that they value these (perhaps this is why young children constantly ask us to 'look at me').
- A love of activity and movement provides emotional benefits throughout life.

Physical health through activity:

- Activity helps the body develop muscles, bones, tendons and nerve connections.
- Movement builds sensory pathways and nerve centres in the brain that co-ordinate and execute the vast array of movement skills needed for life.
- Young children are concentrating on developing a sense of their body and its position in space, in relation to gravity and other objects.
- Moving well brings enjoyment of being active so that children continue to seek activity, laying foundations for attitudes and interests for active lives as runner beans rather than couch potatoes!

Learning through doing and moving:

- Young children need to move in order to learn.
- Development of the brain and the body are completely intertwined and cannot be separated.
- Movement activates the brain to make it ready for new information and learning.
- Movement builds the brain through helping the creation of new nerve connections.
- Concrete experiences felt with the whole body give fuller meaning and lasting memories.
- Expressing new understanding through movement deepens the learning.

Personal and social health through physical play with others:

▶ Movement and physical competences enable the child to join in with what their friends enjoy doing.

▶ They also enable the child to do what others can do, that are socially valued by peers.

▶ Movement helps with learning how to play with others; for instance, simply running together helps friendships form.

▶ Boisterous, physical interactions with others, such as chasing, rough and tumble and being superheroes, are popular ways for boys to play.

WHAT MOVEMENT EXPERIENCES DO YOUNG CHILDREN NEED IN THEIR OUTDOOR PLAY?

Movement and physical activity will be part of nearly everything children do outdoors, as they learn most effectively through doing and moving. We can build upon these desires to maximise the actions and movements that most help physical development. If we know what physical experiences children most need, then we can build these into daily play in *all* areas of provision outside, as well as planning for specific physical activities or having a dedicated area for physical play. It is clear that children need very many opportunities to work on all these areas over time, without rushing them, and this provides a very strong reason why outdoor provision is best available all of the time!

▶ In order to develop the child's sense of balance and how to cope with gravity, they need lots of opportunities to twist, turn, spin and roll and to tilt, tip, jump, bounce, fall, rock and swing. These experiences develop the vestibular organs in the inner ear that tell us where we are in space in relation to the force of gravity. Adults generally do not like these turning and tipping sensations as this system is well developed: children love them because it is very important that they do develop this sensory system! The vestibular sensory system underpins the development of balance and co-ordination, which themselves underpin so much else, so this is a hugely important developmental process for all young children.

▶ To develop an awareness of their body, the feeling of being in it (something we take for granted but actually a vital developmental process) and knowing where their limbs and 'edges' are, children need lots of experiences with pushing, pulling, stretching, hanging, throwing, lifting and carrying, rough and tumble and being wrapped up. These experiences develop the sensors in muscle and skin and all their connections into the brain (this vital sensory system is known as *proprioception* which means 'one's own' and can be likened to internal eyes).

▶ In order to develop a sense of space so that they can move around with ease and control and develop perceptions of distance (how far away something is) and direction, children need lots of chances to fit their body into spaces and to manoeuvre around and amongst objects, including going up and down steps (judging where to place the feet). These experiences link up knowledge about the body (the body awareness and balance inner senses) with the visual sensory system, developing body–eye co-ordination.

▶ Movement that alternately uses each side of the body helps to link up the two sides of the brain by developing the bridge of nerves

▧ **Figure 4.2** Young children need endless opportunities to use their limbs, hands and feet

between them, and this is now known to be very important for a wide array of functions (one of which is following lines of text smoothly across the page when reading). Children need a great deal of opportunity for crawling, clambering, climbing, pedalling, using steps and any other similar 'cross-lateral' activity, from a few months old through into the school years.

▶ For muscle tone and bone density, gross-motor strength, fine manipulative strength and being able to judge the right strength for the task, children need endless opportunities to use their limbs, hands and feet, to lift and carry, push and pull, jump and land, grasp and hold, manipulate and manoeuvre, throw and catch. Since bone density is built up through impact, the general knocks and bumps that happen in energetic outdoor play need to be seen as part of healthy development too.

▶ Being able to move easily through a range of positions, following one movement with another (flexibility and agility), moving at the right speed and being able to judge when to start and stop (timing), being able to make fine adjustments to achieve aim or pick up an object are all advanced physical abilities that depend on masses of opportunity to develop body and spatial sense, balance and co-ordination, integration of these internal senses with sight, touch and hearing, and development of the brain area that plans and carries out motor activity (this is known as praxis, and dyspraxia means difficulty with motor planning). When we consider how much physical development is taking place in the early years of a child's life, it is not at all surprising to find that children are so driven to move and be active in everything that they do!

▶ Resting and relaxation are equally important for physical well-being. Children need to know how to relax, to enjoy being calm and still and to be able to follow the natural cycles of activity and rest that the young human body needs. For children in early years settings this cycle can happen several times even during a half-day session, so comfortable and relaxing places are as important to provide as areas for energetic play. Dens are ideal, as are places to lie down to look at the sky or to sit and chatter. Do not forget though, that sitting still to demand is a very advanced activity for the young child's level of balance and co-ordination development, and most cannot do this for more than a few minutes.

PROVIDING OPPORTUNITIES FOR THE FULL RANGE OF PHYSICAL AND MOVEMENT EXPERIENCES

Features to encourage movement and physical activity

The outdoor space offers most for movement and physical development when it has a variety of features that work together to give a really wide range of experiences. While many features will be permanent and fixed, some can also be created from resources to make temporary and moveable features.

- *Firm, even and relatively flat surfaces* offer opportunities for running, for using bikes and a variety of wheeled vehicles and toys and also for chalking out games, runways or simply a line to balance along. A large area of firm surface is very beneficial in outdoor spaces, but try not to let it dominate your provision; pathways offer a good way to combine hard and soft surfacing.
- *Soft, uneven surfaces* such as grass, smaller areas of sand and bark and even muddy spots, will provide for a whole host of other activities; not least, learning how to move on uneven ground, 'on purpose falling over' and turning on the spot until giddiness makes you fall over.
- *Open areas* allow unobstructed energetic activity without disturbing or knocking into others. Boys especially like to run together or engage in high-energy pretend play with police and baddies or superheroes. An open space encourages movement of all kinds: look for ways for girls to get active too, such as dancing to exciting music.
- *Small spaces*, such as tunnels and hidey-holes in bushes, encourage children to crawl through, hide in and feel how their bodies fit into them. Look for ways of providing small spaces in permanent features, such as the space alongside the shed or underneath a look-out platform, as well as through moveable equipment such as barrels and cardboard boxes.
- *Gradients and different levels* provided by steps, slopes, dips and mounds, are wonderful for meeting children's strong interest in going up and down and their love of being 'high up'. Learning to negotiate steps and sloping ground is very important for young children, who may mainly experience carpets, pavements and

73

shopping malls away from your setting; so do make the most of any you have or look into how you can create 'hilliness' in your outdoor space. Even a small grassy mound, perhaps with a set of steps in one side, will prove very popular for imaginative as well as movement play. A grassy bank is also excellent for rolling down, as most adults will remember.

▶ Curving *pathways and bridges* entice children to follow them, moving from one place to another and learning how to turn themselves or their vehicle around bends. You can enhance the physical challenge in permanent pathways by embedding pebbles and other items into sections, having sections with a gradient and by including traffic-calming-style bumps. Temporary pathways can be made with chalk markings on a hard surface or by using ropes, cones or other small markers: try bamboo canes pushed into soft grass or sand to make an 'in and out' pathway.

▶ *Stepping stones* stimulate children to find different ways of moving along them, such as jumping, hopping, taking giant steps or going in and out between them. They can be set at different distances and heights and can be repositioned occasionally to offer new challenges. There are several resources that can be used by children to make their own stepping-stone challenges: make sure you have suitable items available and that children learn how to use them safely.

▶ *Low walls* with broad tops are very attractive to children who are developing balance and co-ordination. Jumping off provides a tipping and falling experience as well as the control needed to land: walls made to gradually gain in height offer increasing challenges for children to set themselves. Nursery pioneer Margaret McMillan considered 'jumping-off points' to be an important provision in the Kindergarden. As well as making good use of any fixed walls and jumping off places in your space, temporary versions can be made with resources such as milk crates and tyres.

▶ *Traversing walls*, where handholds used for climbing walls are fixed across a length of wall at a height suitable for young children (footholds are around 30cm above the ground), provide marvellous physical experiences that contribute greatly to balance, strength in the back, neck, limbs and hands and to co-ordination across the two sides of the body. Children will learn to judge their own abilities and to stretch them a little more each time: placement of holds can be matched to the children attending the setting. They should always be fitted by a specialist, but most playground equipment companies can supply and fit them to the standards required.

➤ *Walls* have many other uses for physical play so try to keep areas clear for use. Chalking markings onto them, or using poster paint, will give you the option to change the design on a daily basis, whereas permanent markings preclude a different use; so do think carefully about any permanent markings you decide to have done. Attaching hooks to the wall will allow you to hook up baskets as targets for throwing, starting with a large, plastic laundry basket and moving to smaller baskets as children's skills develop.

➤ *Crawling, scrambling, clambering and climbing* are very good for developing co-ordination of the two sides of the body as the alternate use of left and right help to strengthen links across the hemispheres of the growing brain. The pushing and pulling actions in the arms and legs also help to develop body sense

Figure 4.3 Stretching, hanging and clambering develop body and brain

and there is a variety of pressure on the feet. The best features for these activities will have a lot of inherent variety or can be moved and modified to change the movement patterns children are encouraged to make. Large boulders or tree trunks make clambering features that offer marvellous and irregular opportunities which climbing frames often lack. When looking for a fixed climbing frame, select one that offers opportunities to crawl into, under and through small spaces, places to scramble and climb up and over and additional parts that can be used to modify the basic structure. Some settings have climbing frames made from a series of tyres, from huge tractor to small car sizes. Nets, tunnels, tyres, barrels and cardboard boxes also entice children to clamber and crawl.

▶ Poles and horizontal bars help children to develop their body sense through *stretching and hanging*, by their arms and perhaps by hanging up side down. When selecting a climbing frame, look for those with opportunity to hang so as to stretch arms and torso; monkey bars are excellent for this even if children cannot bear their own weight for long. Low, horizontal tree branches can be used in this way if there is room for the child to lift their feet off the ground – first check that the branch is sufficiently sturdy. Twisting round a vertical pole while leaning out and doing 'apple turnovers' over a horizontal bar are popular as the turning action also helps with balance. Being upside down is very effective for developing the balance organs, so do look at ways for children to do this, offering as much support as the child needs. A vertical wooden pole can also become a Maypole with long ribbons.

▶ *Bikes, trikes and other wheeled vehicles* are superb resources for encouraging exactly the kinds of movements and actions that build a child's brain – no wonder children love them so much. They involve pushing and pulling with arms, legs, back and shoulders for development of proprioceptor sensors in muscles, tendons and skin; using both sides of the body alternately for linking up the two sides of the brain; and movements that stimulate the vestibular organs for balance through turning corners and moving fast. Strength, flexibility, hand–eye co-ordination and timing are also amongst the physical benefits from wheeled toys. It is vital however, to select vehicles carefully, to have a good range, to have good challenges for bike use (such as carrying loads and passengers) and to incorporate bike play into well planned role play. Permanent track markings are convenient for adults but lack variety and flexibility of use for children, so do consider making your own to suit the current interests or themes. While bike play can often be a repetitive and even disruptive activity, with thought and planning it can become an area of provision full of imaginative and social potential to match what it can offer for physical development.

Good resources for physical play and what children might do with them

RESOURCES FOR MOVEMENT AND PHYSICAL PLAY

- Ropes both long and short
- Ribbons, bells, scarves
- Music and a CD player
- Bubbles, feathers, leaves to chase
- Chalk
- Brooms, spades and rakes
- Wheelbarrows
- Bikes, ride-upons, carts etc.
- Rocking boats and bowls
- Pushchairs and prams
- Baskets, buckets, bags, pulleys
- Steps and stepping stones
- Small parachute
- Hammock
- Fabric pieces in a variety of sizes
- Balls, beanbags, quoits and hoops
- Milk and bread crates
- Logs and branches

- Small tyres
- Barrels, cardboard boxes and tunnels
- A-frames, ladders, planks

While there are many resources that specifically encourage and support movement and physical play, a lot of the resources you have for other areas of provision will also be very good for this: logs and branches from natural materials; crates and large wooden blocks from construction; spades, rakes and brooms from gardening; scarves and fabric from role play. All aspects of outdoor provision also have great potential for giving children the physical experiences they need, so you can capitalise upon this by providing resources that enhance the physical aspect and by encouraging movement as you support the activity. For example, in the sand area, you can set up a pulley system with ropes and buckets so that children are lifting and pulling heavy weights while they explore sand and play imaginatively. Gardening, woodwork and high-energy role play are also full of movement and physical activity: boys especially are drawn to activity and action. Make sure that children who are less physical have opportunities that are attractive to their interests and styles of play.

There are also lots of movement activities that simply *make use of the space the child is in,* without needing additional resources: jumping and hopping forwards and backwards; rolling down a slope; playing follow-my-leader; skipping, marching, galloping and chasing; turning on the spot until giddy; twisting around an upright pole; crawling on grass or in sand; puddle-jumping; giant-stepping over cracks; making shadow monsters; chasing feathers or falling leaves; kicking through leaf piles; balancing on low walls; walking on all fours; attempting handstands. These are just a few of the many ideas you and your children will come up with!

Collect a list of *games, action rhymes and songs* with movements that work well outdoors: ask parents for ideas as well as all the staff. Type the lists up as prompt sheets and laminate them, attach a loop to hang them up and keep them to hand outdoors, perhaps on a hook in the shed. This way, you will never be short of ideas and end up using the same old few that you or the children can remember on the spot. Aim to introduce a new game or rhyme each week and use it every day so that everyone learns it well enough to use it independently: don't forget to add it to the prompt sheets too.

Add props for the games to your small physical play resource collection, such as frog-shaped beanbags for a game of *Five Little Speckled Frogs* jumping in and out of a blue laundry basket. Wherever possible get children to move themselves as well, so in this example children might jump with the frog into a chalked-out 'pond'. Chalk is indispensable for marking out spaces, runways, tracks, balancing lines, targets and games – children love to create their own so have plenty of chunky playground chalks. Ropes are highly versatile resources and children will find many ways to use them, such as balancing along a long rope laid on the ground, jumping over a wiggling rope, jumping over or playing limbo under a low rope. Many four and five year olds are ready to try skipping, a marvellously developmental activity: provide plenty of soft, short ropes and suggest activities that build the various skills involved, so as to support persistence.

Children love to *dance* and are very responsive to music. Rhythmic movement is an excellent way to make you feel 'in your body' and also to build social relationships by moving in tune with others. Take a transportable CD player outside whenever you can (an external electrical socket is well worth considering, especially in new build or refurbishment) so that you can stimulate movement with a wide range of energetic music. It is virtually impossible for a young child not to run in response to *William Tell*, or to twirl to *Carmen*. Irish jigs and samba music will prompt jumping and turning and African drumming might stimulate stomping and beating. A few simple props, such as ribbons, lengths of floaty fabric and wrist bells are all you need: attaching ribbons, balloons and scarves to soft pony-tail bands allows children to wear them on their wrists. Larger pieces of see-through material stimulate children to run with the cloth covering their head and arms. As children become familiar with the music their movement sequences will build in complexity: try videoing the dances and reviewing them with children later on.

There are many resources for children to *push and pull*: bikes, carts, trailers, scooters, pushchairs and prams, brooms, rakes, long-handled spades, wheelbarrows, pulleys and buckets. Children will also make their own resources, such as by threading a rope through a milk crate to pull around. Encourage them to add weight to these so they can experience friction and to attach ropes to wheeled toys so that they can pull each other along. *Lifting, carrying and manoeuvring* with bags, baskets, buckets, watering cans, wheelbarrows and heavy items such as crates, wooden planks, small tyres and logs gives children stretching, co-ordination and strength-building experiences as well as providing for strong interests in filling, enclosing and

Figure 4.4 Heavy items provide an excellent whole-body workout

transporting. Provide a range of materials to carry, such as sand, pebbles, gravel and water. Den-building, construction, gardening and water play with large resources all involve lots of this kind of physical activity. Make a collection of several types of ball, beanbag and hoops of different sizes, shapes and textures so that children can play with lots of different ways of *throwing, rolling and catching*, gradually building up their skills. By marking on the ground and walls or by providing baskets as targets (see above), children can try all sorts of challenges and games and then invent their own.

Resources such as milk and bread crates and tyres can provide varied opportunities for *balancing, stepping between, bouncing, jumping on and off and teetering* on the edge until you fall off. Provide things to *fit into and crawl through*, such as barrels, tunnels and cardboard boxes. These can also offer *rocking and rolling* experiences for the child inside. Although most early years settings do not have sufficient space for a swing, a hammock can provide a lovely *swinging* sensation, as well as offering a place for relaxation. Staff can also rock children in a blanket or lycra sheet or with a small parachute. *Tipping, spinning and rocking* are all possible with a spinning bowl, a great item for physical play available from many educational and special needs suppliers.

Young children have a deep need for *body contact* and a sense of firm enclosure or containment, for physical as well as psychological development. Provide soft sheets, blankets and fabric pieces that children can wrap around their bodies and small places they can climb into, such as cardboard boxes, barrels and tunnels. Play games with lycra sheets, small parachutes or carpet off-cuts where children are enclosed and gently rolled around according to their own requests (ensure their heads are not covered). This is best done with an adult and just one or two children and for short duration, so that close attention is given to what the individual child is comfortable with – some children love this kind of experience. Suitably sized body balls can also provide body contact with movement. As a team, discuss your approach to rough and tumble play: it has an important developmental role in all social animals, including young humans, and can play a part in your provision for physical play when managed well.

Remember that *enthusiastic, playful adults* can make the best resources! Noticing what the child likes to do and taking the child's lead are the best starting points; children really value your attention and involvement and are also often keen to be given new ideas for play. Encourage interaction, talk and collaboration, introducing the vocabulary of movement with both useful and interesting words, such as slither, gallop and pounce. Giving children such descriptive words does more than simply build vocabulary as it helps them to internalise actions and to plan and carry out future movements. Encourage children's own exploration and creativity in the ways they use the features and resources and pick up on a child's idea to introduce a group to a new way of playing with them. Some children, who may have become timid and risk-averse, will need sensitive support to help them face appropriate risk and challenge positively. Observe and listen closely; plan to enhance and extend as the children seem ready, but remember how much repetition matters too.

HEALTH AND SAFETY CONSIDERATIONS: MANAGING RISK, PROVIDING CHALLENGE

Physical play may feel as if it is full of safety problems as children seek to find challenge and develop their abilities beyond current competencies. The outdoors is a much safer place for movement as the indoors tends to be full of objects and obstacles; many settings actually report lower accident figures outside than inside. The turning point comes when practitioners view the outdoors as a place where children can learn *how to keep themselves safe* through recognising potential harm and knowing how to deal with it. They can also learn how to deal with minor incidents, such as a graze, and to know that the pain is temporary and will go away. It is through such minor knocks and bruises that children learn about hazards and become aware enough to avoid them next time. Children must have challenge that is developmentally appropriate and they must be willing to make attempts, experience failure, frustration and the determination to succeed, followed in due course by the pleasure of feeling capable and competent. These are all important life skills and to deny them to children is a serious mistake with long-lasting effects.

Safety of children outdoors is paramount and our task is to ensure that children have challenge and freedom within a framework of security and safety; that is, an environment that is safe enough, rather than one completely without risk. Most activities that young children do outdoors in early years settings are not likely to involve significant hazards or harm; however, it is vital that we are fully aware and alert, and use thorough risk management processes. We need to assess potential risks and manage them so that children do have the experiences they need without the possibility of serious harm.

A positive approach to risk management will include these steps:

- ▶ Check the outdoor area, its features and resources routinely and frequently, removing damaged items or preventing access: repair or replace as soon as possible;
- ▶ All adults should observe and interact with children's use of features and resources;
- ▶ Know your children – assess the risks for your particular children and try to enable creative physical play rather than limiting opportunities;
- ▶ Use your knowledge of physical development to understand what children are seeking to do in their play and wherever possible find a way of doing it that is safe enough, rather than preventing it;
- ▶ Teach children how to keep themselves safe in physical activities such as climbing – they need to become aware of hazards and risks so that they can learn to manage them safely;
- ▶ Help children become aware of the impact of their actions on others – this will help them learn to look out for their well-being too.

CHILDREN'S BOOKS

Around the World: bicycles Kate Petty (Frances Lincoln with Oxfam 2006)

Bearobics Vic Parker and Emily Bolam (Viking Children's Books 1997)

Bumpus Jumpus Dinosaurumpus! Tony Mitton and Guy Parker-Rees (Orchard Books 2003)

Down by the Cool of the Pool Tony Mitton and Guy Parker-Rees (Orchard Books 2002)

Doing the Animal Bop (book and CD) Jan Ormerod (Oxford University Press 2005)

Five Little Monkeys Zita Newcome (Walker Books 2003) contains over 50 action and counting rhymes, many of which can be used on an active scale outside

Giraffes Can't Dance Giles Andreae and Guy Parker-Rees (Orchard Books 2001)

Rumble in the Jungle (book and CD) Giles Andreae and David Wojtowycz (Orchard Books 2006)

Saturday Night at the Dinosaur Stomp Carol Diggory Shields (Walker Books 1997)

Scaredy Squirrel Melanie Watt (Happy Cat Books 2006)

The Dance of the Dinosaurs Colin and Jacqui Hawkins (Collins Picture Books 2002)

The Dancing Tiger Malachy Doyle, Steve Johnson and Lou Fancher (Simon & Schuster 2005)

We're Going on a Bear Hunt Michael Rosen and Helen Oxenbury (Walker Books 1993)

Where the Wild Things Are Maurice Sendak (Red Fox 2000)

Wiggle and Roar! Rhymes to join in with Julia Donaldson and Nick Sharratt (Macmillan Children's Books 2004)

RHYMES AND MUSIC

Five Little Monkeys Jumping on the Bed

Five Little Speckled Frogs

Head Shoulders Knees and Toes

Here We Go Round the Mulberry Bush

Hickory Dickory Dock

Humpty Dumpty

I'm a Little Indian

In and Out the Dusky Bluebells

One Elephant Went Out to Play

Ten in the Bed

The Grand Old Duke of York

This is the Way the Lady Rides

Walking Through the Jungle

There are many types and pieces of music that work very well outdoors; here are some examples:

Bolero (Ravel)

Carmen (Bizet)

Carmina Burana (Carl Orff)

Carnival of the Animals (Saint-Saens)

The Ride of the Valkyries (Wagner)

The William Tell Overture (Rossini)

African drumming

Bhangra music

Irish and Scottish jigs

Salsa music

FURTHER INFORMATION AND RESOURCES

Community Playthings supplies an excellent range of collaborative wheeled vehicles www.communityplaythings.co.uk

Jabadao The National Centre for Movement, Learning and Health, offers specialised training and resources for movement in the early years www.jabadao.org

Knock on Wood a superb online catalogue of world music and instruments www.knockonwood.co.uk

Spacekraft equipment to meet additional needs www.spacekraft.co.uk

Springy's Playbag, a very good value kit of small resources to support movement and physical play with curriculum materials from Learning through Landscapes (by Jan White), from Davies Sport www.daviessports.co.uk

Choosing Safe Trikes information sheet from Community Playthings www.communityplaythings.com/c/resources/articles/index.htm

The Little Book of Parachute Play Claire Beswick (Featherstone Education 2003)

The Little Books of Playground Games Simon MacDonald (Featherstone Education 2004)

Too Safe for Their Own Good? Helping children learn about risk and life-skills Jennie Lindon (National Children's Bureau 2003)

SUMMARY

► Young children love to move and are strongly driven to develop their physical abilities. We need to fully appreciate just how important and pervasive movement and action is for young children's holistic development.

► Physical play contributes to physical, mental and social health and well-being and some types of movement have particular developmental importance at this age, such as for balance, body awareness and co-ordination.

► Children should be given a great deal of time for movement and physical play outdoors and to have a wide range of experiences.

► All aspects of outdoor provision have opportunities for movement and physical activity – make the most of this for active learning, to increase the range of physical experiences and ensure high motivation for movement.

► The outdoor space offers most for movement and physical development when it has a variety of complementary features that work together to give a really wide range of experiences. Provision can be developed gradually so that all kinds of movements are possible in a range of ways.

► Many of the best resources for supporting physical and movement play are those that settings may already have for other aspects of outdoor provision.

► Effective practitioners delight in sharing children's pleasure and joy of movement and being physically active – adults make great resources for children's physical play.

► Adults should work from children's interests and drives. Children can be trusted to set their own challenges. Interaction, observation, assessment and evaluation are vital in order to plan what to provide or encourage next.

► Children's safety is paramount, but children need appropriate challenge within a framework of security in order to build

85

dispositions for a successful life. We must be fully aware of hazards and work to reduce risks, rather than removing experiences. These are ideal opportunities for helping children learn how to be safe.

Chapter 5

Providing imaginative and creative play outdoors

WHAT THIS CHAPTER IS ABOUT

- What creative and imaginative play does for young children
- Why take creative and imaginative play outdoors?
- Making provision for creative play outdoors

  - Providing for art and mark-making outdoors
  - Providing for weaving, sculpture and woodwork outdoors
  - Providing for music and dance outdoors
  - Providing for imaginative play, stories and performance outdoors

- Making the most of creative and imaginative play
- Children's books
- Further information and resources

I am enough of an artist to draw freely upon my imagination. Imagination is more important than knowledge. Knowledge is limited. Imagination encircles the world.

Albert Einstein

The creation of something new is not accomplished by the intellect alone but by the play instinct. The creative mind plays with the object it loves.

C.J. Jung

WHAT CREATIVE AND IMAGINATIVE PLAY DOES FOR YOUNG CHILDREN

Provision for creative play is one of the most important ingredients in the early years since creativity is so fundamental to our lives, both as children and later as adults. Being able to think creatively – analysing a situation and coming up with new ideas or actions – supports the dispositions needed for learning and life: resourcefulness, positive thinking, having a go, experimentation, persistence, innovation, thinking outside the box and the ability to express thoughts and ideas. Children need to grow up believing that they are creative, being comfortable with uncertainty and happy to work at finding solutions. These are the life skills needed for the twenty-first century, in which change is certain.

It is clear that one of the major functions children's brains are developing from three to five years of age and beyond is the ability to imagine and to use imagination to play with ideas and feelings. Imaginative 'make-believe' play develops the young brain in the areas of symbolic and abstract thought and allows children to replay their experiences so as to process, understand and internalise them. It allows them to take on different ways of behaving so that they can try out roles and ways of interacting; it enables them to explore other people's minds and thoughts. Imaginative play is very important for emotional well-being, and one of the main ways children interact with each other is through shared pretend play. Young children think and communicate best through story and make-believe activity, so they access other areas of the curriculum best through this narrative mode.

Imagination and creativity go hand in hand; we need to be able to imagine in our mind's eye in order to come up with new ideas or see new ways of combining existing ideas. The 'impression–expression' cycle enables understanding by allowing the child's mind to process images of new, real experiences through expressing feelings and thoughts in a personal way, without the pressure of an end-product. Playful, imaginative activity is the bedrock of our ability to be spontaneous, creative and expressive.

Creative, aesthetic and expressive play covers a wide range of opportunities and can be part of most experiences. It includes mark-making, art, drawing, design, construction, problem-solving, music, dance, performance, make-believe play, story-telling and books. Spontaneous play and expression is made possible through setting up a 'generous' environment with lots of potential, providing continuous access to resources, being flexible in planning and ensuring that children know what is there and how it can be made use of. The basic materials must be always available as part of long-term planning so that children build up their exploration of them, leading to unexpected and innovative, truly creative, use. Shorter-term planning will introduce new contexts, new materials, new skills taught by an adult and new provocations. What these actually are should emerge from watching and listening to the children.

WHY TAKE CREATIVE AND IMAGINATIVE PLAY OUTDOORS?

The nature of the outdoors gives children opportunities to engage with creative play in ways not really possible indoors, so this aspect of outdoor provision can significantly enhance and extend children's creative experiences. Many children are simply more relaxed outside, finding it a more liberating, flexible and spontaneous play environment. The greater space gives freedom for movement and large-scale working: there is room to work in 3D, with large materials and in groups. There seems to be more freedom for inventiveness and new ideas. The possibility to be active, noisy, multi-sensory and messy responds to the way many boys like to play so it is perhaps not surprising to find that boys engage more with areas of provision they do not tend to use indoors, such as mark-making. The outdoors accommodates children's natural exuberance when playing musical instruments, singing or dancing. There are very many 'sparks' for creativity from the natural world, real experiences and the locality around the outdoor space. There are lots of suitable role-play scenarios that work better outside, where they have greater authenticity and meaning. Literary, literacy and numeracy activities should take place outside, associated with active and imaginative play, so that children do not come to see numbers and writing as an indoor 'work' activity rather than a play activity.

If you are looking to develop your outdoor environment, this is an easy and enjoyable place to start and a great way to broaden the curriculum you offer outside. The central objective should be to create the conditions for imagination and creativity: creating places, presenting resources, introducing the provocations or sparks to intrigue and capture interest, and giving time for creative play to emerge and grow deep. Creativity will be expressed and engaged in on a personal level and therefore will be different for each individual child. Creative ideas tend to be emergent – they grow slowly out of exploration and play rather than being decided upon and planned out at the beginning; so playfulness and lots of time outside are key.

There is potential for creative thinking in all aspects of provision outdoors; inspiration, problem-solving and expression are possible in all sorts of places, so do not limit your developments to special creative 'areas'.

MAKING PROVISION FOR CREATIVE PLAY OUTDOORS

Because of the potentially chaotic nature of the creative process, it is important to be prepared for mess and disorder and to be committed to the extra effort involved on the adult's part. A truly creative outdoor environment is more of a work-site than a workshop! To keep this productive, it is most important to have good basic organisation and routines. Organise resources in a way that enables children as well as adults to access what is needed as the need arises. Designate an area in your shed for mobile containers: trolleys, trays, toolboxes, crates and backpacks are all suitable. Labelling both the container and its location on the shelves will help keep things in order; laminated photographs are easiest and most effective for both. Develop an expectation that children will put things back and be fully involved in the tidy-up; you will need to persist until this routine is well established, but older children will be able to guide younger ones. Wheeled trolleys with slide-out plastic trays really help to provide a creative work-shop outside. They can be loaded with mark-making resources, joining materials, paper and small-world resources and easily taken to wherever creative activity is taking place.

Protective clothing is vital so that children stay warm and dry while being free to be inventive and get messy all through the year. Provide old clothes or use rain wear, as aprons will probably not cover enough (legs and feet tend to get messy). Be prepared to wash and dry children and to change clothes. Make sure parents know that this will happen and why; if you make the child's learning visible to them, parents will understand the benefits and work with you. Hand washing will be needed so have a bowl of warm water available: an outdoor sink makes life a lot easier.

Let your ideas for new creative experiences emerge from what you observe children to be interested in. Working from children's interests and ideas leads to fuller involvement and therefore more complex and deeper learning. Be careful not to overwhelm with too many possibilities and make lots of room for repeating the familiar, while every so often introducing something new. The best learning occurs when the two halves of the early years environment join up: take indoor resources outside, bring the stimulus of outside indoors and work across the two using what is different about the outdoors, such as the opportunity to continue on a bigger scale. Experiences outside will spark ideas inside and vice versa.

Providing for art and mark-making outdoors

RESOURCES FOR ART AND MARK-MAKING OUTDOORS

- Trolleys, tool boxes and other mobile containers for resources
- Protective clothing, such as rain wear
- Clipboards
- A variety of paper, wallpaper lining roll
- Big plastic sheeting (from DIY store), white or clear shower curtains, polyester/cotton sheets
- Open up large cardboard boxes to give a big cardboard canvas
- Pegs, duct tape and string
- Pens, charcoal, pencils, small palette sets, pencil crayons, wax crayons (for rubbings), big felt pens
- Lots of chunky chalks, both white and coloured
- Thick and thin paint in bottles ready for squirting, spraying or dripping
- Non-spill paint pots, spray bottles, squirting bottles
- A wide range of brushes from fine up to masonry brushes (as for water play)
- Sponges and other kitchen utensils as paint applicators
- Natural materials augmented with glass beads, coloured and sparkly items
- Recycled materials, such as cardboard boxes and tubes
- Magnifiers for close up observation, A5-sized map-reading sheet magnifier
- Viewing frames made from a sheet of card, kitchen/toilet rolls (to focus perspectives)
- Coloured visors, coloured acetate sheets, safety mirrors
- Cameras

Art, mark-making and drawing outdoors

Any outdoor space has lots of potential for working with materials that make marks in a wide variety of ways. Children can use the ground and surfaces around the area to work on a big scale with the freedom to be messy and inventive. At the other end of the scale, they will notice the fascinating detail in things from the natural and constructed world. Young children will happily work on the floor, so make the most of every surface available, both hard and soft: tarmac, pavement, grass, sand, bark, walls and fences. The vertical surfaces offered by fences and walls are an under-used resource in many outdoor spaces and this dimension is rarely available for children to work on indoors. The big scale enables the child to work with both hands at the same time, to make big movements that cross the body's midline (which is good for brain development), to work alongside another child or to make joint creations. Poster paint and chalk will wash off most walls, but you can also provide surfaces for art work with big boards or pieces of slate. Make boards from marine plywood by painting with emulsion or blackboard paint and coating the back with yacht varnish to reduce warping. Big hooks, such as those made for hanging bikes in a garage,

■ Figure 5.1 Use vertical surfaces for mark-making on a big scale

will fit over standard school fences and make the board removable for storage. Painting a permanent base colour onto brick walls with masonry paint will brighten up the space and provide a good surface for children to add temporary artworks with poster paint: permanent murals may look very nice but they can leave little for the children to work with. Cotton sheets, plain shower curtains and rolls of wallpaper lining make great temporary canvases, both laid on the ground and attached to a fence with pegs.

Boys like to draw, rather than write, and willingly engage in group drawing on the ground with chalks: make sure you have a good supply so that this can develop fully. It is also important to provide small comfortable places where individuals can sit and draw with pencils, crayons and clipboards, having been inspired by something from the world around them: providing several sets of mark-making materials in transportable containers will also support this.

Organising resources for art and mark-making outside

Since art work might take place in many parts of your outdoor space, art materials need to be mobile. They also need to be stored in a way that will keep them well organised and attractively presented, as it is very easy for these materials to become muddled so that they inhibit a high-quality creative process. You will need to teach children to look after the resources, replacing them after use, and give attention to keeping resources refreshed and appealing.

Wheeled trolleys with shallow A3 paper trays can be loaded with paper, home-made booklets, previously prepared proformas relating to the role-play theme, mark-making tools, pegs and so on. Shoe organisers from a home-making store provide pockets for mark-making tools, and some shower curtains also have pockets for bathroom items: these can be tied to a fence near to where children are working. Small plastic tool boxes and those made for storing household cleaning items are just right for containing sets of art tools and bottles of paint. These and backpacks are very appealing to children who are exploring schemas of containment and transporting: make sure they are not too heavy. A milk crate can be a useful container in which to store spray and squirting bottles of ready-mixed paint. Designate shelves in the shed for storing these containers in an accessible way.

Things to work with outside: paint, chalk, drawing and writing

As always, aim to give children experiences that they cannot have indoors. It is useful to note that poster paint washes off more easily with a squirt of washing-up liquid. Provide the paint in sturdy pots, trays and bottles. Splash, spray, squirt, drip and print, and use all sorts of application tools and large brushes. Use it on big surfaces in a liberated way; experiment on a variety of surfaces; use it thick and use it runny, so that it runs down the painting surface; spray water onto it to see how the colours run, spread and merge; paint on both sides of a large plastic sheet at the same time; paint in the rain and on wet surfaces; hand-print onto walls; squish it between two layers of clear plastic sheet; put paint into a puddle for children to go through with bikes and wellies; walk along lining paper with muddy feet.

Use the stimuli of your surroundings to inspire creative art work; for instance, by offering just red and yellow paint in autumn. Tell the inspiring story of Frederick, the mouse who stores up the colours of the summer for the long, cold winter for the other mice: 'and when he told them of the blue periwinkles, the red poppies in the yellow wheat, and the green leaves of the berry bush, they saw the colours as clearly as if they had been painted in their minds' (*Frederick* by Leo Leonni, 1971).

Chalk is an excellent material for use outside, especially as it engages boys in mark-making and the large spaces available on tarmac, pavement and walls encourage children to work together. They might be inspired to make road layouts of considerable complexity, showing their knowledge of the route to nursery or their own locality. Wet chalk behaves in a different way; suggest chalking onto wet surfaces during or after rain. Chalk easily washes off, which children will be happy to do with water and brushes, or they can observe as the rain gradually removes their marks over time.

There are so many things that inspire children to draw outdoors, especially things from the living world. This is where a well-stocked mobile trolley or toolbox is particularly important, so as not to loose the moment. Provide a good range of materials and observe to find out which best support what children want to do – improve your provision accordingly. Join children in this activity so that conversation around the drawing enhances the process – group drawing can be particularly powerful at this age.

Likewise, the outdoors can offer many sparks for writing with real purpose and engagement, even for those who do not tend to write indoors.

The adult role includes being alert and prepared to capture these sparks. Signs, notices and labels are often needed, especially for role play and the growing area; play might require a treasure map, instructions or secret messages; children might want to record birds and insects they have seen or to compile a *Book of Questions and Ideas*.

Things to work with outside: natural materials, elements from the weather and new perspectives

Natural materials lend themselves to creative use, both temporary and permanent: they have intrinsic beauty and can be endlessly manipulated to make patterns, mosaics, pictures, sculptures and shapes on the ground. Add coloured and sparkly items, such as glass beads, to increase the visual and tactile appeal. Large cobbles painted with bright colours and then varnished make lovely resources for pattern-making. Shells and pebbles embedded into plaster, clay or cement can make stepping stones to place amongst plants or across grass.

Use mud, gloop (cornflower with water and food colouring) and slime (soap flakes whisked with water) or shaving foam to sculpt, drip and make marks with sticks and fingers. Use the many opportunities that the weather provides for creative play and mark-making, such as making prints, tracks and patterns in snow with feet, twigs or a broom, 'snow angles' by lying on the ground and models of snow people and animals. Helen Bromley provides a great list of mark-making possibilities from rain, fog, frost, snow, wind and sun in her book *Making My Own Mark* (2006, page 58), and recommends that a laminated copy is kept to hand with a 'weather box'. Shadows are a particularly intriguing phenomenon for creative explorations. For example, children might make shadow shapes with their body, hands and objects on the ground and on walls; chalk around shadow shapes and explore shadow effects such as dappled light under a tree with a camera.

Creativity is also inspired when children are offered new ways of looking at the world. Try looking close-up with magnifiers and home-made viewers created from a kitchen paper roll or a square cut-out of a cardboard frame; being shrunk to the size of an ant with special spectacles; or being up high with telescope or binoculars. Explore the world through large sheets of coloured acetate, looking also at the coloured shadows it creates. Cameras are an excellent way to refocus on familiar things and remember too that children already look at the world in a very different way to adults: listen carefully to what they have to say.

95

Providing for weaving, sculpture and woodwork outdoors

RESOURCES FOR WEAVING, SCULPTURE AND WOODWORK OUTDOORS

- Garden mesh and netting
- Garden trellis and willow panels
- Orange plastic builder's mesh
- Oven trays
- Willow and bamboo garden canes (tape the ends to protect eyes)
- Floristry ribbon, silk ribbons
- A good range of 1m lengths of colourful and shiny fabrics
- Colourful plastic supermarket carrier bags (cut into strips)
- Tinsel and Christmas garlands
- Old CDs, beads, shells and other shiny or attractive items
- Natural materials
- Plastic door screens (from shops such as Evolution)
- A very long rope (old climbing ropes are ideal)
- Cardboard boxes and carpet roll tubes
- Logs, tree trunk slices, branch segments, twigs
- Soft wood (processed and rough)
- Simple woodwork tools, nails and safety goggles

If you have wire-mesh fences around your outdoor space, you have plenty of ready-made canvas for weaving on a grand scale. Young children are often fascinated by the schematic concepts of 'in and out', 'going through' and 'connecting' and this is also a great way to improve the look of your boundaries, especially where the view beyond is unattractive or your outdoor space is too open. Weaving is a good activity for the muscle development needed for writing as well as a satisfying expressive experience. Although some weaving will remain as permanent works of art, there should also be lots of opportunity for temporary weaving with a range of fine and coarse meshes for increasing dexterity: fences around the boundaries, wooden trellis and willow panels, plastic meshes and netting from garden centres. The orange plastic temporary fencing used at building sites is just the right size for small hands, which is easier than weaving into smaller spaces with the fingers. Trellis and willow panels can be worked on from both sides, making ideal partitions to delineate a quiet zone in the outdoor space. For very small outdoor spaces, an oven tray attached to a brick wall sticks out enough for children to weave with strips of fabric, ribbon and crepe paper. Children interested in this kind of activity will find other places for weaving and tying knots, such as the grid on the base of milk and bread crates and the branches of small trees. On a larger scale, garden canes pushed into grass make a very coarse weave: if canes are positioned well apart, children will be able to go in and out themselves as they weave with long ropes, giving an experience they can feel with their whole body. A Maypole made by setting a broom-handle into a bucket of cement and attaching several lengths of colourful floristry ribbon, combines dance with a weaving action. Aim to replace or extend permanent weaving annually, so that new children have taken part; a family weaving day is an excellent way to get unsightly fences covered up.

■ Figure 5.2 Young children are fascinated by 'in and out' and 'going through'

Collect lots of materials for weaving and store in tubs from which children can make their selections: rope, colourful string, tinsel, spun and un-spun wool, strips of fabric, colourful supermarket carriers, florist and silk ribbons, bendy twigs and anything else that can be woven at this scale. Also collect colourful, shiny and natural items that can be threaded or tied into the weaving: old CDs, shells, beads, buttons, leaves and so on.

Decorating items around the outdoor area will also prove very popular. Providing a good selection of tinsel strands in buckets will transform your outdoor area around Christmas time. Decorate a tree with anything that comes to mind by tying things onto branches and twig ends. The strands from ornate plastic door screens (used to deter flies from entering in the summer) are visually pleasing when tied in branches, moving in the wind and making a labyrinth-like area for children to move amongst. Home-made windsocks and banners can be made by tie-dyeing cotton fabric with cold-water dye. Children might also use the fabrics provided for imaginative play to make 'Art Attack' style 'paintings' on the grass.

With the space available outdoors there is plenty of scope for sculpture on a big scale. Willow and bamboo canes, cardboard boxes, cardboard tubes from carpet rolls, wood and other found, natural and recycled materials make excellent resources. Children might use cardboard boxes to make dragon monsters which they can then wear for a dance procession, much like a Chinese Dragon. Many settings have their wood-working bench outside as this links well with other outdoor activities and allows more room to work in and bigger constructions to be made. Ensure children know the rules for safe use and have the necessary skills or the help they need to master new skills.

Providing for music and dance outdoors

RESOURCES FOR MUSIC OUTDOORS

▶ Big plastic and metal containers, buckets

▶ Metal and wooden spoons, sticks, brushes

▶ Lengths of plastic and copper piping in a range of diameters and lengths (from DIY stores)

▶ Funnels, cardboard tubes for megaphones

▶ Tins and pots for shakers

> Old saucepans and lids (school kitchen equipment is ideal)

> Old cutlery, natural materials

> Washing lines

> Wind-chimes

> Large and robust percussion instruments from around the world

> World music on tape or CD, portable player

> Bread crates, stepping stones

Young children need to experience music every day and there is nowhere better than the outdoors for this, where they are liberated to make a high-energy, noisy response and where there is stimulation from the environment itself to make sounds and be musical with their whole body. Musical behaviour can occur anywhere in the outdoor space, so do not confine it to a particular place. However, you might construct some music-making structures in appropriate spots – but bear in mind how noisy they are likely to be! The best approach is to consider how 'musicality' can be incorporated into every part of your space and into as many activities as possible, with singing, dancing and rhythmical movement being an integral part of outdoor play. Make use of the equipment and resources you already have, such as hopping along stepping stones in time to a chant or bouncing along a row of bread crates in a movement sequence. Encourage children to explore their own voice through these too, perhaps by making increasingly higher-pitched noises as they go up the steps of the slide, shouting from the top and making a descending 'wheeee' sound as they slide down. Sticks and wooden or metal spoons can be scraped along the textured surfaces of walls and fences and the voice can be amplified down plastic pipes with funnels at each end or along guttering pipes. Children might explore the sounds they can make by sending objects down plastic guttering tubes and hit the ends with a spongy table tennis bat or flip-flop – different lengths and diameters will produce differently pitched sounds. This could progress into making a giant rain-stick with gravel by sealing both ends.

Simple but effective outdoor instruments are easy to make. Once given the idea, children might make lots of different shakers by putting natural materials inside a range of containers, such as a biscuit tin or flower pot. Encourage them to find out how big and noisy the shakers can be. Collect a few big plastic and metal containers, such as a dustbin or compost bin and upturned buckets, and supply big spoons, brushes and other household utensils for drumming. Try this under a gazebo canopy in heavy rain for a really amazing effect and play African drumming music to the children afterwards! (The *Stomp Out Loud* DVD has a remarkable sequence of drumming in the rain too – see resources at the end of the chapter.) Old pans and lids, the bigger the better, can be hung along a washing line with spoons as strikers – painting them with oil-based paint will increase durability outside and make them attractive. Try making wind-chimes from old cutlery, shells and dried clay pieces to add to those bought from shops. Use *Stomp Out Loud* to spark innovative ideas with the children: the musician/dancers use an amazing range of everyday items such as brooms, drain pipes and buckets to make fantastic, energetic musical rhythms.

In the suggestions made so far, very little money has been needed to make a creative musical environment, but you can augment your provision for music outdoors with a selection of robust world percussion instruments, to be used with vigour and action. There are lots of suitable types of music too, from lively jigs, flamenco, South American, African, carnival and classical to mood music to create an atmosphere for pretend play, such as sounds of the jungle. Collect nursery rhymes for marching and dancing, and songs that you all like to sing, changing the words to fit whatever it is that the children are doing, such as, 'This is the way we slide down the slide . . .' Laminate lists so that you are never short of ideas and singing becomes a part of everyday outdoor play. A portable tape/CD player enables children to listen to music and rhymes in a quiet area outdoors and to record their own voices, performances or sounds around the outdoor environment. Settings that are newly built or refurbished should have an electrical supply installed in their outdoor space.

RESOURCES FOR DANCE OUTDOORS

- ▶ Ribbons, ribbon sticks, bubbles and balloons
- ▶ Feathers and leaves
- ▶ Attractive scarves, pieces of voile fabric
- ▶ Soft pony-tail bands
- ▶ Home-made Maypole

- ► Wrist and ankle bells
- ► Maracas, castanets, hand drums
- ► World music on tape or CD, portable player (see Chapter 4 for suggestions)

Music and dance go together especially strongly for young children, who experience feelings and ideas with their whole body. Be ready to capture the creative sparks that are ignited by being outside. Children might be spontaneously inspired to dance simply by chasing falling leaves on a windy day, by responding to the movements of their shadow on a sunny day or by jumping to catch sparkling bubbles on a bright spring day. They might make animal movements such as rabbits hopping, horses galloping and lions charging. Encourage children to explore highly active movements and to come up with appropriate names for them: children's words might well be more interesting than the 'correct' one, although you can also use this as a playful way to increase their vocabulary. Use exotic words and alliteration, such as *slip*, *slide* and *slither*, as many children of four and five love to play with the sounds of words.

Ensure that your instrument collection includes those that encourage movement and dance, such as wrist and ankle bells, maracas and hand drums, and encourage the exploration of movements to make sounds. Select music from all over the world for its potential to inspire children to run, twirl and leap: *William Tell* and *Carmen* are particularly good for this, as is carnival music. There are many types of world music that are excellent for dance outdoors – explore them with the children and make a collection of the ones that work best. A carnival procession brings together music and dance, perhaps with banners you have made previously. Provide props such as pieces of beautiful and floaty fabric, ribbon sticks and bubbles. Ribbons and lightweight scarves can be tied to pony-tail bands so that children can wear them on their wrists. This is particularly helpful for balloons, to prevent them floating away. Remember that some children are frightened by bursting balloons and that the pieces of rubber can present a choking hazard.

Providing for imaginative play, stories and performance outdoors

RESOURCES FOR IMAGINATIVE PLAY OUTDOORS

- Blankets, sheets
- Pegs, string, rope, pulleys
- Pop-up tent, clothes horse
- Construction materials (see Chapter 6 for suggestions)
- Torches, telephones
- Hats, bags, baskets
- Natural materials
- Soft toys, puppets, dolls
- Pieces of fabric in a range of sizes: large; cape-sized; strips for turbans and belts
- A variety of types of fabric to spark different themes, such as camouflage, white, shiny, blue
- Carpet squares, small rug
- Bikes, carts, transporters
- Short lengths of plastic piping (for fire-fighting or making speaking tubes)
- Cardboard boxes: big and small, cardboard carpet-roll tubes etc.
- Trolley(s) with mark-making resources, joining materials, creative materials, small-world resources
- Specific items to support a particular role-play theme
- Themed sets of small-world resources in suitable containers
- Materials for small-world landscapes, such as flower pots, logs and big stones
- Aggregates for small-world landscapes
- Containers for small-world landscape materials, such as tyres

Imaginative play outdoors

Children between three and five engage in a great deal of imaginative play, starting with imitative pretend play that draws directly on known experiences and developing into complex fantasy play in which scene and story are negotiated by several children playing together, and which takes place in an imaginative space shared between them. Imaginative play is therefore a major ingredient for rich outdoor play provision. This is not difficult because the outdoors is rich in potential for supplying stimulation, contexts and materials for imaginative play of all types. Because of the role of imaginative play in processing real experiences, themes for imaginative play should for the most part come from children's own interests: our task is to know what children want to do and to make an environment that is rich in possibilities to match this. Young children have many of their own themes for imaginative play and, like traditional nursery stories, these derive from the deep concerns and preoccupations of young members of a highly social species: universal themes are belonging, families and friendship; good, bad and power; threats, danger, getting lost and being found. Respond to what you notice has interest or relevance, both through observations and from

■ **Figure 5.3** The outdoors is rich in potential for imaginative play

conversations with parents, and ensure that the play you provide for relates to the cultural contexts of the children in your setting. As an example, while football is an imaginative play activity for many young boys, especially during the World Cup, cricket may be more significant for many Asian boys.

By setting up outdoor provision with an emphasis on spontaneous imaginative play, we lay the ground for children to use their own imaginations and creativity. There is, of course, a place for planned and pre-constructed themes outdoors, but do involve children in making decisions, in collecting materials and in creating the site – they are likely to get far more from this approach than being offered a ready-made play scene. Children can become passive players, expecting a scenario to be provided and so losing a big part of their own imaginative drive and abilities; this has already happened in many parts of modern children's lives. The most effective provision offers resources and places as part of what is continuously available so that as ideas are sparked they can be played out straight away.

Because of the very long list of possible themes for imaginative play outside, it is important that permanent play structures are not too defined. Do not make the mistake of installing an overly preconceived structure: a simple wooden house and/or a basic structure that can be modified and embellished has the most potential and will remain of interest for longer. A small wooden shed can become whatever you want and can easily be changed for a new theme – discuss and decide with the children what kind of place it should be for the current season, and involve them in fitting it out appropriately. Some settings have a real rowing boat, donated after it is no longer water-worthy, and these too have a lot of play potential. Supplement this with temporary structures and lots of resources that children can add to the basic structure for a site with lots of imaginative play value. Even young children are quite able to use their imaginations to transform, and representation is something we want them to do. It is quite likely that some of the limited ability of today's children to play imaginatively, which early years practitioners often remark upon, arises from over-use of preconceived play equipment and toys.

An outdoor space that has plenty of small nooks and crannies where children can feel secret, and several different ground surfaces and heights, will offer much stimulus for imagination; children especially love to be up high and underneath. Plants that children can play amongst, such as grasses, bamboo and willow, give an atmosphere of exotic lands, even if this area is quite small.

Provide den-building resources so that children make the child-sized and private spaces from which pretend and fantasy play often develop. Dens can be used for home play, camping, being an adventurer or explorer and as a bear cave (see Chapter 6).

The best props for imaginative play of all types are flexible and open-ended: children can use them to take on many roles and this also means you need to provide less. Fabric, in a range of colours, textures and sizes, is an excellent prop from which children can make shelters, capes, robes, headdresses and belts. Fabric is also very good at suggesting a theme for the imagination to work on. Select fabrics on the basis of how versatile they are: a large piece of blue could be the sea, a river, a lake or the sky; white might be snow or clouds; something shiny could be treasure, a king's robe, fairy wings or a magician's cloak; camouflage material could be the earth, a cave or the jungle. With a good range of fabric, dressing-up clothes are not really needed, with the exception perhaps of safety jackets and mechanic's overalls. Do, however, collect hats, bags and baskets, and encourage children

Figure 5.4 With fabric, children can make shelters, capes, robes, head dresses and belts

to bring out soft toys and puppets from indoors. Anything made from fabric is best stored indoors, especially through the winter, so organise them in easy-to-move containers. A wicker trunk, a suitcase and a shopping trolley are all ideal and often become part of the play themselves. Lightweight laundry baskets and plastic tubs with handles also work well.

Some planned themes for role play are more suited to the outdoor environment or will extend indoor themes, and there is actually a long list of exciting and meaningful possibilities:

- ▶ Home play, camping, picnic, barbecue, beach, holiday, lighthouse-keeper . . .
- ▶ Garage/mechanic/MOT, car wash, truck/digger, construction site, train engineers . . .
- ▶ Police, fire-fighting, ambulance, road-crossing, painter, window-cleaning, washday . . .
- ▶ Pirates, treasure hunting, boat, castle, fairies, magic carpet, witches/magicians, cave, island, explorer, archaeologist . . .
- ▶ Traditional nursery stories, especially those that take place in a forest . . .
- ▶ Café, drive-through, supermarket, garden centre, market stall, vets, farm . . .
- ▶ Post and parcel delivery service, removals, Father Christmas, railway station, airport runway . . .

If a theme has been particularly successful, keep a list of the additional resources you used, for easy gathering next time. Bike play is well suited to many of these themes so do take the opportunities that arise to extend and enrich children's use of vehicles. Include literacy wherever it makes sense and has meaning, such as booking in for your vehicle's MOT or a police officer recording the number plate of a bike that has transgressed the rules. Give vehicles numbered parking spaces and use carts and baskets to deliver letters and parcels; in December you could have a present-wrapping station indoors and a loading bay outside for a cart transformed into a sleigh. Letters written indoors can also be delivered to posting boxes around the outdoor area with a special post bag.

Another way to support imaginative use of the outdoor area is to make signs, such as supermarket logos, café menu and order pads, delivery times on the post boxes, number plates on bikes, house numbers, and notices such as 'danger men at work', 'buy petrol here', 'smell me', 'this way to the magic dell'. Children might also arrive in the morning to find a 'help me' letter with a problem that needs solving or a treasure map to follow. When children are used to including writing and drawing in their imaginative play, they will want to do their own, so keep a trolley of suitable materials well stocked.

There is also huge potential for small-world imaginative play outside with many little landscapes available everywhere, in sand and soil, in grass and amongst plants. Encourage children to use flower pots, logs and stones to make homes and hills etc. If your space is limited to tarmac, you can also create some extra landscapes by filling tyres with various interesting aggregates, such as white chippings for an arctic landscape or sandstone pebbles for a desert. Grass grown in a soil-filled tyre offers long-grass jungles and short-grass prairies; children will enjoy cutting long grass back with scissors! Keep themed sets of small-world resources in containers that children can easily carry to the place they have chosen to play: dinosaurs, British wildlife, wild animals, arctic animals, domestic/farm animals, mini-beasts, vehicles, play people, fairies and so on. It is better to have a central storage trolley from which children can select than to place sets yourself,

Figure 5.5 The many little landscapes outside inspire small-world play

as children may well come up with more inventive combinations and ideas. Make sure that natural materials are also to hand for this play.

Stories, books and story-telling outdoors

RESOURCES FOR STORIES, BOOKS, STORY-TELLING OUTDOORS

- ▶ Collections of books and rhymes related to the main aspects of provision outdoors
- ▶ Collections of books and poems that read well outside and are good starting points for further activity
- ▶ Collections of books and poems that support predictable interests from being outside
- ▶ Audio books and portable player
- ▶ Baskets and other containers for small selections that can be carried by children
- ▶ Picnic rug, cushions, carpet squares, tent, parasol, large umbrella, hammock

For most young children between three and five, story makes more sense than the real world. Putting something in terms of a narrative seems to help them both to understand and to put their own ideas into words: this is why we deal with complex issues such as feelings and guidelines for behaviour with puppets and books. It also shows in children's love of books and story-telling, both of which should be provided for outside just as much as inside. For some children, having story read outside, rather than indoors, makes them more likely to participate. Some stories are perfect for telling and exploring outside; the setting may reflect the context of the story and being outside creates an atmosphere and a place for re-enacting it.

Books make excellent starting points for much further activity, especially imaginative play (see the lists of children's books in each chapter). In *Exercising Muscles and Minds* (2003, pages 67–69), Marjorie Ouvry sets out an extensive array of possible lines of development in every area of learning from *Mrs Mopple's Washing Line*. In *Making My Own Mark* (2006, pages

55–57), literacy expert Helen Bromley gives an analysis of possible learning outdoors for language, reading and writing that could be built into long-term plans starting from the book *Where's Julius?* (John Burningham, 2001).

Your outdoor area needs lots of places for looking at and sharing books, for telling stories, acting them out and adapting them and for composing your own stories together. Books are most effective outside with very small groups, perhaps just one or two children with an adult, so you can choose the spot depending on the book. The most important conditions are comfort and atmosphere, such as near or amongst plants for a jungle feel. Ideal places to share stories are in a swing seat or hammock, under an arbour or pergola, on a picnic blanket or magic carpet, under a big umbrella in the rain or a parasol in the sun. To create a book area, provide small collections in a basket or tool-box with a blanket and cushions or inside a tent or den. A large tractor tyre also makes an excellent story-telling circle that can also be used for discussions, review and eating snacks together.

Throughout this book I have listed children's books and rhymes for supporting the main aspects of provision outdoors, because we know that children are strongly engaged by these themes. Books and poems for outdoors should also be selected as they are especially good for reading outside because of the atmosphere in this environment or because we can capitalise on the greater freedom for an active response (such as *We're Going on a Bear Hunt* by Michael Rosen and Helen Oxenbury, 2001); because they make good starting points for imaginative and creative play outdoors (such as *Frederick* by Leo Leonni, 1971) and because they support predictable interests arising from being outdoors, such as mini-beasts, wind, snow, vehicles, friendship and superheroes. Helen Bromley lists her ten top books for inspiring writing through play outdoors in *Making my Own Mark* (2006, page 54) and these are included in the suggested books below, with kind permission. Do not forget to include audio books with a portable player so that children can take one to their preferred spot to listen, submerging themselves in the story's atmosphere.

Performance and drama outdoors

> ## RESOURCES FOR PERFORMANCE AND DRAMA OUTDOORS
>
> ▶ Puppets, soft toys, dolls
>
> ▶ A pair of old curtains
>
> ▶ Hats, bags, jewellery
>
> ▶ Instruments, microphone or Karaoke machine
>
> ▶ Bread crates, wooden pallet, carpet tiles

Story-telling, play with puppets, singing and dancing can all extend into a performance for those children who enjoy having an audience, but at this age they are likely to be fairly spontaneous and short. A simple stage can be made from an up-turned bread crate, or a wooden pallet is just the right size for a larger and more permanent one. Curtains hung from tree branches make a good puppet theatre, or you can mark out a screen with chalk on a wall for a shadow performance. Role-play props will provide fabric, hats, bags and jewellery for dressing up and a microphone will inspire imitation of modern singers. Seating can be made from milk crates and carpet tiles will make them more comfortable! Position mark-making materials nearby, in case posters or tickets are wanted.

MAKING THE MOST OF CREATIVE AND IMAGINATIVE PLAY

A camera is a really useful resource for this aspect of provision, especially as many creative 'products' outdoors are ephemeral and cannot be kept or taken home. Recording the process of creation allows you to examine children's involvement and plan next steps with other staff, to share and value it with parents and to review the experience and stimulate new ideas with children. Children love to see themselves in images and can become quite skilled with a camera. Progress to a digital camera as soon as you feel they can use it properly as this opens up the art of photography itself.

The need for children to have plenty of time cannot be over emphasised. Good-quality creative and imaginative play sessions will not develop if time outdoors is short and children do not know whether they will be able to go outside the next day. They must know that they will have access to long periods outdoors every day for their interests to develop and involvement to become deep. Opportunity for repetition and trial-and-error gives time for ideas to emerge and for mastery of new skills; they also build concentration and persistence. Children may well want to return to a project later in the day or the next day, so the question for us is, how can we leave some projects outside so that children can continue to develop them?

The adult role is very sensitive in supporting imaginative play. Young children love to have an adult's involvement but they will often let you take over the direction of play, which is all too easy to do. An attentive adult who is seeking to understand what is going on in the children's minds will be able to make small suggestions or provide further resources to support and continue the play. There is a need for young children to be taught new skills or ideas so that they can expand their own repertoire for future use. If the role-play theme is not very familiar, the adult will need to model role behaviour, language and play ideas to make it a success for the children (Wingate Children's Centre's *Outdoor Banking* DVD is an excellent example of this). Above all, it is important to value children's creative and imaginative play outdoors highly, using observation opportunities to find out what is in or on a child's mind, as well as what they can do for formative and summative assessments.

It is important to consider the needs of every individual in making provision for this area, and how they might interact. Older children are the very best tutors for younger children's play, and this is particularly so with imaginative play. Consider how you can have mixed ages in outdoor play, as so much is lost by having separate play sessions. Evaluate your provision frequently to ensure that experiences relate to all cultures within the setting and be alert to stereotyping. Gender differences are very noticeable in imaginative play outside, where boys tend to be much more boisterous than girls: how much do we value what is actually happening in rough and tumble or superhero play and are girl's needs fully met outside?

CHILDREN'S BOOKS

Creative Play

Angel Pavement Quentin Blake (Red Fox 2004)

Chidi only Likes Blue: an African book of colours Ifeoma Onyefulu (Frances Lincoln 1997)

Follow the Line Simone Lia (Mammouth 2002)

Frederick Leo Leonni (Hodder and Stoughton 1971)

Gregory and the Magic Line Dawn Piggott (Orion 2003)

Mister Seahorse Eric Carle (Puffin Books 2004)

Noisy Parade: a hullabaloo safari Jakki Wood (Francis Lincoln 2002)

The Dot Peter Reynolds (Walker Books 2004)

The Shape Game Anthony Browne (Corgi Children's Books 2004)

Imaginative Play

Blue Rabbit and the Runaway Wheel Chris Wormwell (Red Fox 2001)

Dear Zoo Rod Campbell (Campbell Books 2001)

Harry and the Dinosaurs Romp in the Swamp Ian Whybrow and Adrian Reynolds (Penguin Books 2007)

If We Had a Sailboat Jonathan Emmett and Adrian Reynolds (Oxford University Press 2006)

Mr Grumpy's Outing John Burningham (Red Fox 2001)

Someone Bigger Jonathan Emmett and Adrian Reynolds (Oxford University Press 2003)

The Green Ship Quentin Blake (Red Fox 2000)

The Gruffalo Julia Donaldson and Axel Scheffler (Macmillan Children's Books 1999)

The Shopping Basket John Burningham (Red Fox 1992)

The Train Ride June Crebbin and Stephen Lambert (Walker Books 1996)

Tim, Ted and the Pirates Ian Whybrow and Russell Ayto (Harper Collins Children's Books 2006)

Treasure Hunt Alan Ahlberg and Gillian Tyler (Walker Books 2003)

Walking Through the Jungle Julie Lacome (Walker Books 1995)

We're Going on a Bear Hunt Michael Rosen and Helen Oxenbury (Walker Books 2001)

Where's Julius? John Burningham (Red Fox 2001)

FURTHER INFORMATION AND RESOURCES

Art

Prints of works of art with outdoor relevance: calendars are a great source (individual prints can be laminated for use outside); high street art shops, such as Athena, have quite cheap prints (keep the plastic film on for outdoor use); download prints from internet art sites. There are very many possible works; here are some examples:

- *Landscapes*, such as Wolf Kahn, Paul Powis (*Seeing a Whisper*), Giuliana Lazzerini (*Village at Sunset*), Vincent Van Gogh (*Cornfield with Cypresses*), John Miller (*Moon over the Bay*), H. Leung (*Mountain Glory*)
- *Colour*, such as Jackson Pollack, Wassily Kandinsky (*Farbstudie Quadrate*); Gustav Klimt (*Pear Tree*), Laffanki (*Silent Valley*), Nel Whatmore (*Colour Field 3*)
- *Children playing outside*, such as L.S. Lowry (*On the Sands*), Pieter Bruegel (*Children's Games*)
- *Mosaics*, such as the works of Antoni Gaudi

www.artnet.com information on artists and art movements

www.artgroup.com for online mail order prints, includes prints from the Tate

www.allposters.co.uk for online mail order posters, includes landscapes and fine art

Calendars and postcards with colour, art and photography themes: there are many high-quality images available in card and book shops, such as the *Nouvelles Images* range www.nouvellesimages.com

Andy Goldsworthy: a collaboration with nature Andy Goldsworthy (Harry N Abrams Inc 1998) Andy Goldsworthy is an artist who works with natural materials in the landscape in a most remarkable way: fabulous colour photographs

The earth from above calendar from Graphique de France artistic aerial photography of landscape forms and features www.graphiquedefrance.com

Mindstretchers for weaving materials www.mindstretchers.co.uk

Children, Art, Artists: the expressive languages of children, the artistic language of Alberto Burri Reggio Children (Reggio Children 2004) has a fabulous section on children's use of natural materials

Everything Has a Shadow, Except Ants (Reggio Children 1999) available from Sightlines Initiative www.sightlines-initiative.com

It Is Not a Bird Yet: the drama of drawing Ursula Kolbe (Peppinot Press 2005) www.sightlines-initiative.com

Making My Own Mark: play and writing Helen Bromley (British Association for Early Childhood Education 2006)

Nature's Playground Fiona Danks and Jo Schofield (Frances Lincoln 2006) includes many inspiring possible creative opportunities

Rapunzel's Supermarket: about young children and their art Ursula Kolbe (Peppinot Press 2001) from www.sightlines-initiative.com

The Little Book of Messy Play Sally Featherstone (Featherstone Education 2002)

Music

Knock on Wood (online catalogue) for world music and instruments www.knockonwood.co.uk

Sounds Like Playing: music and the early years curriculum Marjorie Ouvry (British Association for Early Childhood Education 2004)

Stomp Out Loud DVD Musician-dancers use everyday items to make the most amazing music sounds and rhythms (Vine 1997)

The Little Book of Junk Music Simon MacDonald (Featherstone Education 2004)

The Little Book of Nursery Rhymes Sally Featherstone and Linda Caroe (Featherstone Education 2002)

Imaginative play

Bad Guys Don't Have Birthdays: fantasy play at four Vivian Gussin Paley (The University of Chicago Press 1988)

Early Excellence has a very extensive range of small world resources www.earlyexcellence.com

Exercising Muscles and Minds: outdoor play and early years curriculum Marjorie Ouvry (National Children's Bureau 2003)

Look the Trees are on Fire Rising Sun Woodland Preschool DVD shows very imaginative use of weekly visits to a woodland site and how adults planned for 'provocations', from sightlines-initiative.com

Outdoor Banking DVD Wingate Children's Centre Tel 01429 837572, explores how adults can support a new role-play theme outdoors

The Little Book of Prop Boxes for Role Play Ann Roberts (Featherstone Education 2001)

SUMMARY

▶ Creativity and imagination go hand in hand and are very important for young children's well-being and all-round development.

▶ Taking provision for imagination and creativity outside significantly extends and enriches children's experiences because of what the outdoors has to offer that is not available indoors: the outdoors offers a wonderful environment for imaginative and creative play.

▶ Creative experiences outdoors include mark-making, art, drawing, weaving, sculpture, woodwork, music, dance, pretend play, small-world play, story-telling, books and performance. The outdoors can offer rich and relevant opportunities in all these areas of experience that are quite different from what can be offered indoors.

▶ Plan for a generous environment outdoors with lots of stimulus and opportunity, continuous access to relevant resources, an emphasis on spontaneity and flexibility in planning and provision.

▶ Since creativity is not a tidy process, a truly creative outdoor environment is more like a work-site and likely to be somewhat chaotic and messy, so good basic organisation and routines are important.

▶ Children should have opportunities for extensive creative activity and play outside all through the year. Keeping warm and comfortable is vital and rain wear works well.

▶ The basic resources for this area of provision need not cost much and can be easily collected into mobile containers for children to take to where they need them.

▶ The most effective resources for the development and use of imagination and expression are open-ended and versatile, so that they can be used by the child to represent whatever he or she wants. Outdoor provision can play a significant role in supporting the development of such representational and symbolic thinking.

▶ The best places and equipment for imaginative play are simple and flexible in use, allowing them to be modified to suit children's current play needs. Provision for imaginative play should balance the introduction of planned role-play scenarios with children's own spontaneous play themes.

▶ Books and story-sharing have an important place in outdoor provision, where relevance, context and atmosphere can be greatly enhanced.

Chapter 6

Providing for construction and den play outdoors

WHAT THIS CHAPTER IS ABOUT

▶ Why construction is so effective outdoors
▶ Resources for construction play outdoors
▶ Some of the best things to construct with
▶ Storing and organising resources for construction outdoors
▶ Supporting play in and with structures children have made
▶ Getting the most out of construction play across the curriculum
▶ Gender differences in construction play outdoors
▶ Evaluating your provision for construction play
▶ Children's books, rhymes and songs
▶ Further information and resources

Young children's most powerful learning is accompanied by the expression of wonder, excitement, enjoyment, fun and pleasure.

Marion Dowling

WHY CONSTRUCTION IS SO EFFECTIVE OUTDOORS

Construction activity is of huge interest for young children, increasing greatly in complexity from three to five years. The big ideas we can see children working on during construction play can be summed up as 'how does the world work?' and 'how do I fit into it?' and both are of vital interest to our avid young meaning-makers. Because children will have plenty of space, freedom and stimuli outdoors, construction play is greatly extended by offering it as a main ingredient of your outdoor provision and children can do lots more to explore these big questions. As you will see in this chapter, construction, building and making outdoors offers huge potential for learning and development in all aspects of the curriculum for the early years. It is especially successful because it is full of moving and doing, so that it meets the way young children learn best. The greater space for construction means that we can offer big resources which invite children to work communally on a big scale. The high levels of activity and action, together with removal of constraints upon noise and mess, allows boys to engage in higher levels of social, co-operative play and dramatic play than they do indoors (see *Outdoor Play in the Early Years* by Helen Bilton, 2002, page 70). Do remember that taking things apart is an important aspect of construction, as 'de-constructing' is a good way to find out how things are put together.

A special kind of construction is the wonderful world of den-building and this is especially important in outdoor provision. Young children have a great need for small, nurturing spaces and they can be constructed on grass, sand and tarmac as well as amongst bushes. Dens seem to have a special appeal and to generate particular ways of playing, especially when they offer a feeling of being out of sight and a place from which to look out.

■ Figure 6.1 The wonderful world of den play

Outdoor spaces so often lack softness and comfort, so this is a really effective way to add places for emotional security and where quieter or daunted children feel able to play. The spaces made in den and other construction play can then become whatever the child's powerfully imaginative mind wants them to be.

Construction can take place in many ways and in most parts of outdoor spaces: different surfaces and features will inspire different types of construction, from tiny to grand scale, and spontaneous play may occur in unexpected places. To get the most out of this fantastic activity, consider how to encourage relevant kinds of construction in all aspects of your outdoor provision; for example, making cane wigwams for the growing runner beans. So that you do not confine construction to a particular time, type or place in your outdoor area, you will need to offer a good range of suitable resources on a continuous basis and in mobile containers available from a central workshop-style base (which is likely to be your shed), adding extra resources and enhancement activities as interest arises.

RESOURCES FOR CONSTRUCTION PLAY OUTDOORS

There are many great resources that will invite children to build and make outdoors. As always, think about how the construction play you are providing for outside complements, links to and extends the experiences children are having indoors and at home. You will want to build upon previous experience while offering opportunities that are new and that make the most of what the outdoors brings: space and scale – from tiny to grand; features, surfaces and spaces that make a very different environment to indoors; materials and resources that cannot be offered indoors; stimuli from around and beyond the outdoor space, from home or from the local area.

Open-ended resources that do not have a fixed purpose for play and which can be used in many ways by children will offer lots of potential for building and construction. These resources will also be used for many other activities and will therefore constitute the mainstays of your continuous provision outdoors. Large items, such as boxes, crates and guttering will encourage group construction, but remember to provide resources for small-scale and individual constructions too.

When selecting the resources you will make continuously available, try to ensure that children always have opportunities to:

- Construct on a grand scale, such as creating bridges, towers and obstacle courses;
- Construct for real purposes, such as making temporary seating with tyres and planks;
- Make dens and secret spaces;
- Make tiny structures, such as with twigs and pebbles;
- Make things to use, such as woodwork or instruments;
- Construct in many places, using features such as sand, soil, slopes and the climbing frame;
- Construct in role-play scenarios, such as a builder's yard in the sand pit with ropes and pulleys;
- Once made, play in or with their constructions.

SOME OF THE BEST THINGS TO CONSTRUCT WITH

RESOURCES FOR CONSTRUCTION OUTDOORS

- Milk and bread crates (check for broken parts)
- Tyres (ensure clean and no metal protrusions)
- Large wooden blocks (from *Community Playthings* and *NES Arnold*)
- Washing powder boxes (taped closed ensuring no loose powder)
- Large plastic flower pots
- Cardboard boxes – use as 3D and opened out as large sheets
- Bricks (small-size real bricks – ensure edges are not sharp)
- Soft play blocks
- Plastic drums (such as water dispenser bottles; any container that previously held chemicals must be rigorously cleaned and sealed)
- Guttering, down-pipes, cardboard carpet-roll tubes
- Bamboo canes (tape ends to protect eyes), broom handles, lengths of 1in diameter doweling
- Roll of plastic-coated garden mesh fencing (from garden centres)
- Wood off-cuts, tree trunk slices, branches cut into short lengths
- Short lengths of planking for outdoor decking

> Clothes airers/clothes horse (old-fashioned wooden ones are ideal, but remove hinges to avoid trapped fingers)

> Large pieces of fabric, blankets, sheets, net and other curtains, lengths of muslin

> Tarpaulin, camouflage net (from army surplus stores), big plastic sheet (from a DIY store)

> Small parachute

> Carpet tiles or pieces, plastic-backed picnic blanket, beach mat

> Ropes, washing line, pulleys

> Plastic cones

> Buckets, wheelbarrows, bikes and carts for transporting materials

> Natural materials, such as shells, pebbles, sticks etc.

> Joining materials, such as string, masking and parcel tape, carpet or duct tape, treasury tags, pegs etc. (in a trolley or tool box for ease of use)

> Woodwork bench and tools, safety glasses

> Hooks in walls and fences to provide attachment points for ropes

STORING AND ORGANISING RESOURCES FOR CONSTRUCTION OUTDOORS

Children need to know what is available for construction, how the materials can be used (and any limitations on this), where to find particular resources and where to return them to when finished. If the resources can cope with getting wet, such as crates and guttering, they can be stacked outside, leaving valuable space in your shed: an occasional wash down with the hose will delight children interested in water play. Fabric items are best stored indoors to prevent damp and mildew, so find containers that make transporting them outside easy: a laundry basket might be just the thing as children can easily see and access the contents and can work together to carry it. Resources made of cardboard are easy to replace, so can be stored in a shed and allowed to gradually deteriorate, being used in different ways as they fall apart. In contrast, expensive wooden blocks need a good wheeled trolley as you will want to store these indoors.

■ **Figure 6.2** Bread crates make superb construction resources

Make sure resources are stored in the shed in a way that makes them as easy as possible to find, bring out and return – how you do this will depend on the size and shape of the items. As well as crates and laundry baskets on shelves, consider hooks for individual items and bins for long items; elastic cords attached to hooks in the wall can help to keep items in place. Laminated photographs attached to containers will not only show children what is in the container, but will also remind them of things made previously or give them new ideas for constructions.

SUPPORTING PLAY IN AND WITH STRUCTURES CHILDREN HAVE MADE

So much more will be gained for both well-being and learning if children have plenty of opportunity to develop other play with their constructions: time and supportive adults are perhaps the resources children most need for really effective construction play outside. Children are unlikely to invest effort in constructing something unless they feel that they will have time to make the use of it they have in mind, and short periods of play outdoors are just not conducive to deep and complex play. When children have lots of time to build dens, they have been observed to build a basic structure, then play with it for a while, then to decorate, extend or otherwise embellish their dens and then to play in it some more. This cycle of construction and imaginative play can continue over time if children have opportunities to return to their structure over the day or even over the week, so it is well worth taking a new look at your provision to see if constructions must always be cleared away.

The range of constructions children might make outdoors and the variety of activities they may then want to follow through in or with them is surprisingly wide, but many of the resources you have available for other aspects of provision will offer what is needed:

- Role-play scenarios, such as a builders' yard with construction hats, cones and wheeled vehicles or home DIY with tools and tape-measure in a toolbox;
- Home play and fantasy play, adding a torch and binoculars to your resources for imaginative play;
- Small-world resources for play with small-scale structures created, such as play people, fairies, trucks, dinosaurs and natural materials – a wheeled trolley with pull-out drawers is ideal for making these resources available;
- Cushions and blankets for making a comfortable place to rest;
- Puppets and books to tell stories in the special place made;
- Real food for snack in the den;
- Pulleys (from hardware and sailing shops) and ropes, with paper and pens to make message systems or transport other items to and from the den, or with buckets to add to the building site;
- Clipboards to plan the construction or to draw and map out the resulting structure;
- Mark-making materials to make signs (such as the name of the den or safety advice such as 'Danger! – hole in road'), directions or pathways etc. Again, a trolley with pull-out drawers kitted out with pens, chalk, paper and joining materials allows these materials to be taken wherever they are required;
- Things to decorate the construction or den with, such as ribbons, strips of fabric, big felt pens, chalk, paint, old CDs, natural materials, wool etc.;
- A performance with instruments made or a place outside, such as the branches of a tree, to decorate with woodwork items made;

► Real building materials to explore closely, together with examples provided by wooden and brick buildings in the outdoor space or locality;

► A camera for children and adults to take photographs of the work in progress – these could be displayed or made into books which children will return to many times.

GETTING THE MOST OUT OF CONSTRUCTION PLAY ACROSS THE CURRICULUM

The best kind of provision supports all areas of the child's development through holistic, joined-up experiences, and a good judge of the value of an experience is to examine how broadly it covers the curriculum. Construction outdoors is a truly holistic aspect of provision, especially when children have plenty of time to develop their play and it is supported by adults who can notice, capture and build upon what children are showing interest in. Let's take a look at some of the potential for learning and development that well-supported construction play has to offer the child.

Emotional and social development

When children are following their own interests and satisfying their strong urge to find out by taking apart and putting together, they develop positive

■ Figure 6.3 The range of constructions children make outdoors is surprisingly wide

123

dispositions such as taking an interest, being involved, making plans, concentrating, trying things out, making mistakes and persisting with challenge and difficulty. They will need just the right support from adults to successfully build these desirable approaches to life.

Because there are many opportunities for big-scale construction and group role play, building partners will be learning how to work together, negotiate and collaborate. Play in dens is especially important for supporting emotional well-being outdoors, giving children soft places with feelings of enclosure, security and nurture, and a place where they can regulate the amount of interaction they have with others.

Communication and the foundations of literacy

In both the communal and the solitary activities of construction there are lots of motivational contexts for the use of language, language development and the introduction of new vocabulary. Children often welcome the (sensitive) help of adults to achieve their plans, so staff will find many opportunities both to support conversation and discussion with open-ended questions as they work together and to model language use by responding to children's comments. All construction activity can provoke episodes of sustained, shared talk and thinking between children and with adults because of the shared purpose. Big-scale, group construction is especially rich in provoking the use of language for both communication and thinking and a whole host of sophisticated communication skills: turning the visual idea into words, articulating and describing what the idea is, conveying it to others so that they understand, negotiating the plan, problem-solving in order to achieve the plan and the complex language used when playing imaginatively in the construction made. In addition, there is all the new vocabulary specific to building, materials and structures, such as brick, wall, corner, build, strong, wobbly, inside, balance, fall-down, mortar and so on.

Construction play is also full of reasons to make marks or use emergent writing, such as drawing a diagram of the construction or making a sign to warn that hard hats must be worn. There will be many stories to make up and many more to read – construction has strong links to all kinds of imaginative play, and factual books showing how things are made are of particular interest to boys.

Movement and physical development

Construction can be a very active and physical occupation, especially with large construction items and when boys are involved. Children will be lifting, carrying, bending, placing, stretching, manoeuvring, holding, pulling and pushing; all of which are excellent for developing muscles, strength, co-ordination, body awareness, spatial awareness and motor planning and control (praxis). They will be using their fingers for joining, developing dexterity and hand–eye co-ordination, and they will also be using the senses in a joined up way, so helping integration of sensory pathways in the brain. Remember too that all this energetic activity can be balanced by having a cosy snack or story in the den that has just been made.

Understanding of how the world works, including mathematical thinking

Construction play helps children in their quest to know about their world: what it is made up of, what things do and what they can make them do. They can explore and experiment with materials and how they can be put together and taken apart. While constructing they will be discovering 'what happens if . . .' and about cause and effect ('If I do this, then that happens'). When building a tower or a wall they can, just like true scientists, ask questions, have ideas about how things work (theories), experiment with those ideas, predict what will happen, and then refine their theories with this new information.

During construction activity children will be getting first-hand and 'felt' meanings for lots of concepts, such as gravity, weight, balance and friction. They will be learning design skills and technical knowledge about how to join things together, and they will have to identify and solve problems when their construction ideas do not work and to evaluate the structure once they have succeeded in making it. Make use of your locality as it is quite likely that some building work is going on nearby. Take the children out frequently to watch, take photographs and discuss what is happening, then create a relevant role-play scenario if the children show interest. Be sure to make the most of the experiences children bring from home. You might have a small expert if some kind of construction is going on or a parent or carer works in the industry. For example, a three year old who laid all the books out side by side on the ground explained that he was 'building a patio like Daddy'.

Many of the major schemas that occupy young children are naturally supported in construction activity, such as connecting, transporting, lines and trajectories, in and out, going through a boundary, enclosure and containment. A group of children with similar or compatible schematic interests are likely to work well together on a large construction and those with very different interests might well come into conflict, so being 'schema aware' will be very useful in planning and providing useful support! Schemas have strong relationships to mathematical development and construction play provides endless opportunities to really get a feel for shape and boundaries, space, size and fit, position (inside, under, behind), matching and sorting, comparison (more, less, longer, thicker) and measurement (how high, how long), and to use the relevant vocabulary when it means something to the children. A child can get a strong, felt meaning of space and 'inside' when their body is surrounded by a construction they have just made for themselves.

Creative and expressive development

While deeply involved in constructing, logical and creative thinking are truly working side by side in the child's mind. Much construction play involves creative thinking: exploring the way materials can be used, using previous knowledge to apply to a new situation and putting things together to create new combinations. Children are also visualising and then expressing their ideas, thoughts and feelings, whether it be with the overall plan of what it is they want to build or with a specific problem that needs to be worked out. Sometimes, children will have an idea to start with and can make drawings to help them plan it. Often though, ideas will emerge as children start to play since creativity usually grows better in a playful and non-demanding situation. Many children will want to make drawings of constructions they have enjoyed making.

There is a great deal of stimulus for the child's imagination while they are engaged in building or making and much potential for imaginative or creative play to follow on, such as fantasy play, role-play and playing instruments made. Observe your children attentively to catch the sparks that will help you fire further creative activity.

Figure 6.4 Logical and creative thinking are working side by side in the child's mind

GENDER DIFFERENCES IN CONSTRUCTION PLAY OUTDOORS

You are likely to notice significant differences in the way boys and girls undertake construction activity. Research into gender differences in children's use of the outdoors showed that boys played with the more active equipment and girls tended to stay with the quieter home-type play (Cullen 1993 in Bilton 2002). Boys tended to modify the landscape more frequently while girls' modifications were more likely to be in their imaginations, such as turning branches into shelves. Boys tended to build the outer parts of a building – the walls, windows and roofs – and girls dealt with the interior design – tables, chairs and decorations. Significantly, when boys came across girls building they would take over and the girls would become subservient (Hart 1978 in Bilton 2002). These findings show how vital it is to observe, evaluate and adjust both what you provide and how you support it to ensure girls as well as boys have opportunities that appeal to them and that allow them to retain leading roles. Girls often enjoy having an adult to talk to, so

127

are more likely to engage with construction activities, such as woodwork, where an adult is fully involved.

EVALUATING YOUR PROVISION FOR CONSTRUCTION PLAY

It is very useful to closely monitor what is happening in particular areas of your outdoor provision so that you can periodically evaluate how well that aspect is working for all your children, and consider how it might be made more effective. As an example, some questions to ask yourselves about your outdoor construction play, perhaps at a staff meeting, are given below to help you think about just one of the main ingredients of outdoor provision. It can be enormously beneficial to take a similar in-depth look at each of the main ingredients of outdoor provision, spread out over the year. Different members of staff could take the lead on different aspects, so as to spread the task and give everyone a stake in the provision outside.

First, use observations everyone has made about what children do (or do not do) and how their play is stimulated and supported to consider how effective current provision is. Then discuss and agree what you could do to further develop it. Do not forget to ask the children for their thoughts, feelings and ideas, as this will greatly increase your understanding of the play, give you ideas for development you as adults would not have thought of, and give the children a great sense of responsibility and ownership of the outdoor provision.

- Which children get involved in construction in your outdoor area? What is it that appeals to those who are engaged?
- Are there some who do not find it interesting: why might this be and what can you do to engage them?
- Which resources work particularly well for construction: would more of these be valuable?
- Which construction activities and resources interest boys and which interest girls: how could you increase their interest and involvement?
- What aspects of the early years curriculum are being strongly supported through your construction activities: how could you share this with parents?
- How could you further develop construction opportunities to bring in other areas of learning in motivational ways?

- ▶ Do all staff enjoy supporting construction activity and do they find it easy to take an appropriate and effective role: what could you do to help this?
- ▶ Does construction activity interfere with any other aspect of your outdoor provision: what needs to be done to improve this?
- ▶ Are there any other issues arising from observations, comments from home and discussions with the children?

CHILDREN'S BOOKS

Can't You Sleep Little Bear? Martin Waddell (Walker Books 2005)

Mr Bear's Picnic Debi Gliori (Orchard Books 2001)

Once Upon a Tide Tony Mitton and Selina Young (Random House Children's Books 2005)

Picnic Mick Inkpen (Hodder Children's Books, Little Kippers 2001)

Polly's Picnic Richard Hamilton (Bloomsbury Children's Books 2003)

Rosy's Visitors Judy Hindley and Helen Craig (Walker Books 2002)

Sally's Secret Shirley Hughes (Red Fox 1992)

Sleep Tight, Little Bear Martin Wadell (Walker Books 2005)

The Lighthouse Keeper's Lunch Ronda and David Armitage (Scholastic Children's Books 1994)

The Three Little Wolves and the Big Bag Pig Eugene Trivizas and Helen Oxenbury (Egmont Books 2003)

We're Going on a Bear Hunt Michael Rosen and Helen Oxenbury (Walker Books 2001)

Whatever Next? Jill Murphy (Macmillan Children's Books 1995)

There are many appropriate factual books, such as on how things are made, machines and buildings. Try Heinemann www.heinemann.co.uk/library and Dorling Kindersley www.dorlingkindersley-uk.co.uk

DIY and building magazines with lots of full colour images.

RHYMES AND SONGS

Hickory Dickory Dock

Humpty Dumpty

London Bridge Is Falling Down

Peter Hammers with One Hammer

The Animals Went in Two by Two

FURTHER INFORMATION AND RESOURCES

Exploring Learning: young children and blockplay Pat Gura (ed.) (Paul Chapman 1992)

Look the Trees Are on Fire The Rising Sun Woodland Preschool DVD from Sightlines Initiative has good sequences of children constructing in the woodland and following on back at nursery www.sightlines-initiative.com

Outdoor Play in the Early Years: management and innovation Helen Bilton (David Fulton 2002)

Supporting Young Children's Sustained Shared Thinking: an exploration A training DVD produced by Marion Dowling for the British Association for Early Childhood Education, includes an excellent sequence of children making a willow structure. Available from Early Education www.early-education. org.uk

The Little Book of Bricks and Boxes Clare Beswick (Featherstone Education 2003)

SUMMARY

- ▶ Construction play is of great interest to young children as it helps them to find out about their world in the ways they most like to learn: through moving, doing and using their whole body.

- ▶ A wide range of construction activities are possible outdoors, stimulated and supported by the special nature of the outdoor environment.

- ▶ Children need lots of time to construct and then to play in or with the structures they have made; short periods of outdoor play do not allow children to get deeply involved in such activity.

- ▶ Well resourced and supported construction play is a remarkably holistic experience for children, with the potential to support a great deal of learning in all areas of the early years curriculum.

- ▶ Construction play can take place in many ways and in most parts of the outdoor space, and can also be part of other aspects of provision outdoors, including constructing for real and useful purposes.

- ▶ The best resources for construction play outdoors are open-ended and versatile. Big resources encourage collaborative construction activity on a large scale.

► Resources for construction play should be constantly available to support both planned and spontaneous ideas and interests, and are best organised in mobile containers in a central workshop-style base.

► Adults can take many roles in construction play from interacting closely in order to scaffold children's language, thinking and skills, to supporting 'from a distance' through observation and planning: this range of roles is vital for making the most of this fantastic aspect of outdoor provision.

► Keeping a close eye on what children are doing and saying so that provision can be evaluated is very important in ensuring that provision outdoors is as good as it can be.

Index